College Blues

A (First) Novel by

Dan Henricson

Loose Change Publishing

First Edition Published 2020

ISBN 978-0-646-83030-8

Copyright © Dan Henricson

Apart from any fair dealings for the purposes of private study, research, criticism or review, as permitted under the Copyright Act, no part may be

reproduced by any process without written permission.
Inquiries should be addressed to the author.

Printed in Australia by Ingram-Spark, Victoria

Contents

Part 1. Just Keep Running 1

    A (Very Brief) History of the Royal Military College 4

    Cadet Classes and Companies. 11

    A Brief Guide to Army Tactics. 27

    The Balloon Commander Joke 46

Part 2. Tempus Fugit 69

    Mooseheads Tavern aka The Moose 75

    The Room in a Room 92

Part 3. The Home Stretch 143

    The Last Man Standing Game 173

Epilogue 217

Thanks 221

College Phrases, Acronyms and Military Terms 223

Dedication

Oi Cadet!

Someone once told me that twenty years can seem like a really long time, or no time at all. I know that when I was a cadet, I had no idea how I'd get through each week, let alone where I'd be two decades later.

But now as I look back on my time at the College, I realize that when I left, I took more than just a set of rank slides and a handful of memories with me. Of the many lessons the College taught me, the most important had nothing to do with being on time, keeping fit or leading by example. Yet, it has become one of the cornerstones of my life and has helped me to get through the many challenges life has thrown at me since then.

'Look after your mates' is more than just a catch-phrase to anyone who has ever worn a uniform, it is a way of life. Even after our last day of service, this principal lives on in the way we look after our family, friends and those around us.

So, to all who have served, firstly, I thank you for your service. But as importantly, thank you for continuing the great military tradition of looking after your mates. All day, every day.

Staff Cadet 8100

Part 1. Just Keep Running

"Just keep running," I remember muttering to myself between breaths.

The hill seemed steeper and the distance to the top a little longer each time we attempted it.

"That's four! One more to go!" screamed a large, muscled man in a red and white singlet from above us, his face looking like it would explode at any moment. As I touched the wall of the gym, I hoped this would be the last time we'd have to attempt the hill today. Looking down, I saw my classmates spread out along the well-worn trail from the 'bottom-of-the-hill', a street sign next to the footpath, to the hard stand out front of the gymnasium.

At the front of the group were the super fit cadets who had ran track and field or cross-country at high school. They made it look easy in the summer heat and looked smug as they sprinted past everyone else on their way up the hill. In the middle of the pack were the hard workers, those who'd played a bit of sport or were lucky enough to have been born with good genetics. At the back of the pack were those that weren't designed with running in mind or had ignored doing any physical training before getting to the College.

My feet thumped against the scorching pavement as I got to the bottom of the hill. Reaching out for the street sign that marked the turn-around point I reached my arm out at the last second to catch it and spun around to face the ascent again. Looking up at the hill ahead of me, I could see it crawling with a patchwork of multi-colored t-shirts and red faces. Throwing myself forward, I saw a couple of cadets take a tumble on the way down.

"Leave 'em where they are! If they're dead, they can stay there!" the man in the red and white singlet yelled from above.

I leant into the hill once more and threw my arms forward in the hope that they would propel me upward just that little bit more. I puffed and panted alongside my classmates until we eventually reached the hard stand and jostled back into our ranks. In all we made up three lines of cadets standing shoulder-to-shoulder, heels together, arms squeezed against our sides and eyes facing dead ahead. We sweated and sucked in as much air as we could, waiting for whatever punishment was next.

"Bloody hell, if this keeps up, I'm never getting out of here," the bloke next to me whispered in between breaths.

Forty long minutes later, after what felt like a thousand pushups, pull-ups, sit-ups, jumps, twists and sprints around the gym we were a sweating mess. As we stood there puffing and panting, the Physical Training Instructors, or PTI's, had barely raised a sweat. Their hair remained perfect, their tanned and muscled bodies remained relaxed under their red and white singlets. In comparison, we looked like a bunch of out of shape bank tellers who had just run a marathon. The senior PTI stepped forward to address us.

"Remember this, as junior officer's, you are expected to be fitter than the men and women you lead," he shouted as he walked along the front rank. Occasionally he paused and glared at the red faces in front of him.

"Which means you have a long way to go. Some of you cannot even do five pull-ups! I'm disgusted at the lot of you. You have a long way to go before you can expect to march out of here. You will be seeing us a lot, because remember this – you will not graduate unless you pass PT. And we will be here watching you."

He stopped at the end of the rank, turned to face us and braced himself up.

"Class... Dismissed!"

As one, we turned to the right, took three steps and then broke into a run. Without looking at our watches, we knew we were already late. I pushed through the bodies in front of me to run alongside a couple of cadets wearing the same-colored t-shirt as me. Three abreast, all wearing the same yellow t-shirt with our last name emblazoned across the front, we looked like something out of a Monty Python skit. To my left was Hobbes, to my right was Watts.

"Shit boys, that was punishing," I puffed between steps.

"Yeah mate, I'm rooted. Another one of those and I'm off to the RAP," joked Watts, his red face sweating and smiling at the same time.

"Shut-up you blokes, the Drilly's hut is just around the corner," someone behind us hissed.

We quietened down, as we could see the Drill instructors hut fast approaching. As we jogged past the hut, we looked for any movement that might indicate the possibility of a Drill Sergeants lurking in the shadows. We survived and continued the remainder of the journey back to the company lines tight lipped.

Arriving at the front door of Long Tan company, we burst through the doors and rushed to our rooms. I shook my head and swore as I realized how much time we had before our next class. We only had five minutes to shower, hide our sweaty gear, get dressed into a clean uniform and 're-appear' out front of the lines.

"Could be worse," I muttered to myself as I grabbed a towel and raced off to the showers.

A (Very Brief) History of the Royal Military College

The Royal Military College was opened in 1911 at the site of a sheep station known as Duntroon. It's mission was simple, to prepare officers for service and the first class graduated just in time to be dispatched at the outbreak of the first World War. Of the first class of 117, 40 died during service in the war. After the war, the College was moved to Sydney in 1931, where it was known as Victoria Barracks, Duntroon Wing until 1936 when it returned to Canberra. Its role remains the same, to produce young officers who are capable of leading soldiers into battle. Where-ever and when-ever that may be.

...

"One minute to go you guys, hurry up!" someone yelled from down the hall.

I was still sweating buckets and had only just grabbed my pants out of the cupboard. Although my sweat stained gear was still strewn across the room, I wasn't stressed. At this stage of the training, I knew that inside of sixty seconds I could slip into uniform shirt, fold it into my trousers, grab my folder and throw my hat on. As 2nd class cadets, we were masters of the 'split' and could easily change uniforms in minutes.

I did a quick check in the mirror before I tucked my books under my arm and headed out to join my classmates. Instinctively, we double-checked each other to make sure we hadn't forgotten anything before marching off for our tactics lesson. As we marched towards the lecture hall, our shirts stuck to our backs from the summer head and we didn't waste any time trying to get into the air-conditioned building. We hustled in through the double doors and raced to find a seat under the watchful gaze of our instructor. Tactics instructors were some of the most experienced officers on the staff and tactics was like a religion to them. As such, there were no allowances for tardiness, nor were there any jokes during tactics instruction.

In the middle of the lecture theatre, the instructors stood motionless; his lone shape silhouetted against the dull glow of the ceiling lights. He waited until the class was seated and the last rustle of books had stopped. He glanced around the room and then at his watch. Captain Schwartz had little tolerance for those who didn't respect the importance of punctuality. It was rumored that he set his watch twice a day, including weekends.

"My watch says, 1034 (ten thirty-four)," he said, pausing for effect, "this class was due to commence at 1030."

He looked up and scanned the room for effect. Silence.

"So, as you have taken four minutes off my day, I will take four minutes off your day. And the next time you are all late, I will make sure you all make up for it on the weekend. Does everyone understand me?"

"Yes Sir," came the muffled response from across the room.

"Time is of the essence ladies and gentlemen. As an officer, you are expected to be on time at all times. At some stage in your career, lives may depend on it, so you better sort yourselves out. Now, get out your enemy pams," he said sharply and made his way to the lectern.

He spent the next hour lecturing us on the equipment and tactics that our enemy would employ when we encountered them. In order to graduate, we would not only have to master our own tactics, but also those of our fictitious enemy, the Mussorians. So, our initial tactics lessons were spent studying their weapons, the structure of their units, how they would deploy on the battlefield and most importantly, how to draw them onto our battle maps. This information was contained in the shelf full of folders, or pams, that each of us had been issued when we marched in. From what we read, the Mussorian forces were tough, well organized and well equipped. Exactly where the land of Mussoria might be was not so clear but we learned not to ask those questions and focused on learning what we were told.

As the lesson wore on, the cool blasts from the air-conditioner dried my sweaty shirt and started to give me the chills. I scribbled furiously as Captain Schwartz walked across the mockup battlefield that was spread across the floor and explained the ways the enemy would operate when we faced them. By the end of the class, my head was spinning with weapon ranges, field symbols and enemy formations. The lesson concluded with Captain Schwartz returning to his place at the lectern and fixing us with a steely gaze.

"Righto you lot, make sure you spend some time reviewing your enemy disposition and weapon ranges before this week's exercise. You do not want to fail your first exercise. Make sure you grab a copy of the problem before you leave. Duty Cadet."

The Duty Cadet marched down from his place and called us to attention.

"Class!"

We braced up in our seats, hands clenched in fists and arms straight out in front of us on our desks.

"Dismissed!"

Heading Captain Schwartz's warning, we made sure that we grabbed a copy of the 'pink' and 'green' sheets that contained the information we needed for the exercise on the way out of the room. As I barreled down the stairs, I shoved my pen into my issued green folder and stuffed the sheets in beside it. Behind me, I could hear Watts puffing as we stepped into the summer heat.

"Jesus, how many of these bloody Mussorians are there?! We'll be in the shit if we ever have to fight the lot of them," he said as adjusted his hat.

"I'm with you mate. Ain't it lucky that they don't exist," I replied and we both grinned.

Arriving at the mess, we bounded up the stairs and into the main dining room. With all of the classes in barracks, the dining room a heaving mass of bodies. Whilst Army cooks were often the brunt of many jokes, the food was always good at the mess, as the College made sure we were all provided with enough calories to get through the long days of training. Today was no exception and there were trays full of steak, chicken, potatoes, pasta, vegetables and, being summer, there was some new sort of salad.

"Seriously, who actually eats salad?" Watts said as he piled food onto his plate until it threatened to spill over the sides.

"Apparently, it's part of a balanced diet," quipped Hobbes from behind him.

"My diet is perfectly balanced. I have steak and chicken." "And three helpings of ice-cream," I added.

"Ice cream doesn't count, everyone knows that!" Watts grinned and hustled off to look for a seat.

We scanned the room looking for an empty table. Looking around the hall, we could see tables full of senior cadets who ate merrily and eyed off the junior cadets as they walked by. We skirted around the senior cadets and found a seat amongst our classmates at the back of the room.

"Does anyone wonder how the Mussorian Army somehow managed to sneak onto the Majura range? I would have thought we would have seen something in the papers before they got here," Logan said with a sly grin.

"I'm with you mate, it does seem like a lot of effort just to get into bit of a dust up with the Corps of Staff Cadets," Olly replied.

"But I bet they're shaking in their boots now they know you're here," Watts added through a mouthful of food.

As we ate, we argued about which set of facts and figures we should focus on for the upcoming exercise. The conversation bounced back and forth, with each of us trying to prove we knew that little bit more than the others. With my plate almost clean, I checked my watch and held my hand up with two fingers raised.

"Mess parade in two minutes."

The rest of the table consulted their watches and commenced finishing up the last scraps on their plate.

The weekly mess parade was compulsory for all cadets in barracks and we joined the crowd as they hustled out to the small parade ground behind the mess. Whilst it was conducted in the manner of most other parades, it was slightly less formal and was run by the senior cadets without any staff present. After hustling onto the hard stand, we formed up in our company groups and waited for the Cadet Duty Officer to bring us to attention.

"Corps, Atten-shun!"

In unison, we raised our boots to regulation height before slamming them into the ground. The clatter of our boots on the pavement echoed off the buildings.

The President of the Mess Committee, or PMC, marched crisply out to the front of the parade and halted sharply.

"Parade, stand at … ease!" he barked

"It has come to my attention that some cadets have been abusing their mess privileges and have been taking alcohol back to their rooms from the mess."

As he spoke his beady eyes darted around the ranks, as if to identify the culprits.

"If I catch those responsible for this sort of behavior, they will be spending their next couple of weekends on the parade ground! As junior officers …" he trailed on for the next minute, berating us all for our lack of officer qualities and the need to be role models for our troops. He scanned the ranks again when he finished before bracing himself up.

"That is all. Duty Officer!" he yelled.

The Duty Officer remained in place and opened his notebook.

"From the BSM. A reminder that the barbers will be open this Thursday from 1600 through until 1800 hours. He recommends that everyone has look at the state of their haircuts and make sure they are compliant with dress regulations by Monday. Extras will follow for those who are not compliant."

He read through a handful of other notices before pausing as a sly grin appeared. He looked up to the parade and then back to his notebook.

"From the Adjutant. Nothing!"

A snigger rose from the ranks. The adjutant never had any messages, but the Duty Officer was still required to report this important fact. The humor of this was not lost on those of us prone to seeing the funnier side of College life. Unsurprisingly this rarely included any of the cadet hierarchy.

"Paraaaade! Atten-shun!"

We promptly raised our boots to the regulation height again before slamming them onto the pavement. The Duty Officer looked around briefly to check we were all in the correct position.

"Paraaaade. Faaaall-out!"

As one, we made a sharp right turn and took three steps before breaking off in the direction of our next lesson or assigned activity.

"Man, I don't get this shit with the hierarchy. Most of them were doing the same thing six months ago, so I don't see what makes them so special all of a sudden," I grumbled as we marched back to the lines.

My classmates had heard this rant from me many times before and had grown accustomed to ignoring it. Most of them managed to fly under the radar when it came to the senior cadets and saw no need to rock the boat. I was at the opposite end of the spectrum and had done my best to ingratiate myself to most of the senior cadets in our company within the first few weeks. I questioned their approach whenever I was asked, which wasn't very often, and took umbrage at the way they thought they were superior to us.

"Mate, you need to chill out and play the game a bit. They're just being assholes, because that's what they think they have to do. They'll be gone in less than six months, so just ignore them and stay out of their way," Hobbes said cheerfully.

"Would love to mate, but I can't cop it. Anyway, what's the worst they can do, take my birthday off me?!" I replied with a grin.

"Your choice, but you know you'll lose that battle. I'm sure you're already in the bad books with most of the hierarchy. Not to mention the company Drilly."

"Bring it on. I eat extra's for breakfast."

Hobbes shook his head, and I knew he was right. But, like the rest of my classmates, I was young and over-confident, so I wanted to dig my heels in. Regardless of whether it was a good idea or not.

Dan Henricson

Cadet Classes and Companies.

Training at the College is divided up into six-month blocks, or 'classes', starting in 3rd class and finishing in 1st class. This practice dates back to the opening of the College, when the course took four years to complete, with each year representing a 'class'. This changed in the late 80's to three classes of six months per class, however, the practice of calling junior cadets 'fourthies' remains in remembrance of the time when there were four classes.

When they arrive at the College, cadets are allocated to one of the five companies. The companies are named after the famous battles of the twentieth century and include Long-Tan, Kapyong, Kokoda, Alamein and Gallipoli. It is rare that a cadet will get moved between companies during training and so often the closest bonds they form are with their classmates in their company.

Each cadet company is run by an OC (Officer Commanding), who is supported by a Company Drill Sergeant or "Drilly". Company OC's and Drilly's are often hand-picked from operational units, as a posting to the College was seen as good for their promotional chances. The structure of Corps of Staff Cadets 'regiment' is illustrated below.

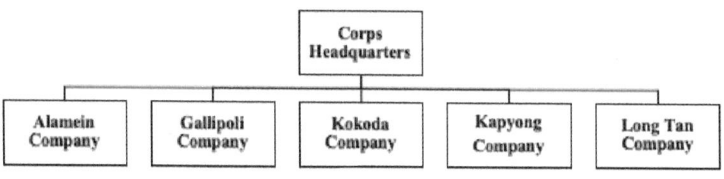

...

Long Tan Company's OC was Captain Sala. He was an ex-soldier who had worked his way up through the ranks before becoming an officer and was the very definition of what we called 'green'. Once you met Captain Sala, you quickly learned that there wasn't much about the Army that he didn't know. To him, the Army was not only his profession, but his sole purpose for living. As such, he believed his role as an OC was simple: to ensure we mastered the art of warfare, developed the proper decorum and at all times lived up to the expectations set for commissioned officers. This meant that some of us would not make it and he made no bones about this, reminding us frequently of the percentage of cadets who did not graduate. He rarely handed out praise and anyone who did not meet his rigid standards pretty quickly made their way onto the company Drill Sergeant's 'shit list'.

After marching back to the lines, I started to split into fatigues for the afternoon's drill lesson. As I was half-way through pulling on my trousers, I noticed one of the Drilly's handwritten notes sitting on my desk. Under my desk I also noticed my sweaty PT gear that I had failed to hid sufficiently after the mornings session. "Come see me" it said in neat print above his trademark signature. It seemed that the OC and the Drilly had pulled another 'random' inspection of my room whilst we'd been at our tactics lesson.

"Fuck me," I whispered.

In the very least this would mean another arse chewing and few less hours of spare time this week. But there was nothing I could do about it, so I shrugged my shoulders and rushed down to join my classmates who were forming up in front of the company.

On the march to the parade ground, I whispered, "anyone else get a visit from the Drilly this morning?"

"Yeah, me too. Looks like we're back on the round-about," Vinny said out from beside me.

"Quiet you lot, head and eyes to the front," hissed the Company Orderly, as he proudly punched his arms through their full range of motion in a demonstration of his commitment to the art of marching seriously.

Arriving at the Drill Wing, we halted and waited. The Drill instructors were experienced senior soldiers, most of them with twenty years of service behind them. Like the company staff, an instructional posting to the College was good for their promotional chances as it gave them a chance to master the various parade disciplines.

"Well, what are you lot waiting for?!" boomed a voice from behind us.

"Stop 'dicking about' you lot and go get your swords!"

Without turning around, we knew it was the Drill Wing Sergeant Major (DWSM), Warrant Officer Fritz, who was a master of the art of sneaking up on unsuspecting cadets and a cranky old bugger at the best of times. With him as our instructor we knew that that there would be no laughs today and that we'd better get cracking if we were to avoid another tongue lashing. We scrambled into the store under the drill hut to grab the ceremonial swords we'd need for the lesson. As we hustled back onto the parade ground, I heard the clang of metal on bitumen that accompanied someone dropping their sword.

"Cadet fuck-knuckle, what do you think you are fucking doing?" the DWSM yelled, moustache bristling in annoyance.

"Ahh, sorry Sarge. I just ahh, dropped it," said one of the cadets that we had taken to calling Possum. As he fumbled with the sword and scabbard, he was totally unaware of his blunder and thus, was completely unprepared for what was going to come next.

"What did you just call me?!" the DWSM yelled.

If he had been a cartoon character, steam would have been coming out of his ears. The Possum stood up and tried to gather himself, realizing his error but unsure what to do to correct it. His only response was to pull himself up into the attention position and look straight ahead. He looked like some sort of animal caught in the headlights, hence the nickname.

"What is my rank cadet?!" the DWSM spat as he strode to face him.

The Possum remained silent, blankly starring into the distance. In his mind we guessed he was hoping the DWSM would forget about it and let him get back to his day. Of course, that was not going to happen. The DWSM waited menacingly, jaw twitching and fists balled.

"I did not spend the last twenty years of my life working my way up to warrant officer to have some cadet call me 'sarge'! As a young officer you will be expected to recognize the rank of your fellow officers and soldiers in the barracks and in the field and show them the proper respect. Your soldiers will only follow you out of curiosity for so long young cadet, so you had best get your head screwed on correctly. Come see me after the lesson! The rest of you – carry on and be quick about it!"

We sprang into action and jostled ourselves into a single rank at the edge of the parade ground. As we stood waiting for the DWSM, the sunlight reflected off our swords, throwing little patterns of light onto the hot parade ground that was already warming the soles of our boots. With the DWSM as our instructor our focus improved considerably. As he barked commands, we snapped our swords into the various positions that we'd need to master. Each movement was accompanied by a whispered, "wah-two-three," to ensure we stayed in time with the rest of our classmates. Over time, these catch words became so well drilled into us that it provided the rhythm for almost everything else we did during training, from weapons drills, to drinking toasts and many after-hours exploits as well. At the end of the lesson, we (carefully) returned our swords to the store while the Possum was given a solid tongue lashing by the DWSM and a couple of extra check-parades for his troubles.

As we marched back to the lines Hobbes whispered, "Jeez Poss, I thought he was going to shove that sword fair up your date, and you were going to end up looking like a Possum kebab."

The rest of us giggled until the Company Orderly 'shushed' us again.

After arriving back at the company, we drifted back to our rooms happy for the fact that training was over for the day. For most cadets, that brought about a sigh of relief as it meant you had nothing scheduled to do until the next days parade. Looking around the corps on any given afternoon, you'd find cadets working on their fitness, cleaning their gear, reading up on enemy tactics, or occasionally engaging in a stealthy bit of fraternization. Whilst there was always something to prepare for, most cadets didn't need much encouragement to join their mates for a brew and the chance to sit around and talk about the day's events. However, if you were on one of the instructors 'shit lists', your spare time quickly disappeared. Over the years, the instructors had developed an arsenal of activities to chew up any spare time we had, including various types of parades, inspections, re-tests and exercises. We were told this was to help us to get better at managing our time and space, but most of us knew it was simply because we'd pissed someone off.

First on the list of jobs that you ended up with was a few extra days of Company Orderly. This was a bit of a stuff about but didn't require much more than being up a bit earlier and possibly having to have an extra uniform ready for morning flag routine. Next came the various inspections that often followed one of the parades, where your gear was identified as Not Up to Standard, or NUTS as we knew it. You could be picked up for being NUTS at just about anything that you wore, did or had in your room. This included things like uniform NUTS, rifle NUTS and room NUTS. Most of these inspections occurred in the lines with the senior cadets, and if you failed you would be deemed NUTS-NUTS and end up back for another inspection at some stage. Next were 'check parades', which were simply that, a check to make sure you were there. They were part of the daily routine for anyone who was confined to barracks or on restriction of privileges (ROPs) but could also be handed out for any number of minor infractions of the rules (often referred to as Timing-NUTS). You normally had to stuff up pretty badly to end up on ROPs, but there were plenty of rules to break at the College, so there was usually at least one cadet who was confined to barracks most weeks. If you were on someone's 'shit list' there was a better than average chance you'd end up with at least a couple of inspection each week and possibly a 'checkie' thrown in for good measure too. As I'd finished my last inspections a couple of weeks ago, I knew a visit to the company Drilly's office that afternoon was more than likely to result in a few more the coming week.

The Long Tan Drilly's office was situated at the end of the company, right next to the OC's office. If the OC was in, you would often arouse a comment as you walked past his door just so you knew he had seen you. "Ahh cadet such and-such, here to see the drilly again are you?" he'd offer as you marched past. Today the door was closed, and I wondered if he might have been off somewhere having a go at being human for a change. Looking around, I noticed I was first in line for a change and positioned myself outside the Drilly's door.

Our company Drill Sergeant was much like the OC. He was humorless and completely dedicated to his role of keeping the cadets in his charge in line. Whilst some company Drilly's were occasionally seen smiling and engaging in a bit of light conversation with the cadets, Sergeant Zimburger was not one to let himself relax at any time. He was a Military Policeman, which already made him unlikely to have many friends according to the sentiment of the ex-soldiers amongst the cadet class. Like water and oil, we didn't mix and within the first couple of weeks of arriving I had already earned the top spot on his 'shit list'.

Inside his office, I could hear him banging away furiously on the issued computer on his desk. I leaned forward and knocked on the door.

"Who is it?" he called.

"Cadet Rickson, Sergeant."

"Ahhh, Cadet Rickson. What a pleasant surprise. Come on in," he replied smugly and leaned back in his chair.

I marched into his office and halted on the red X that was marked on the floor in front of his desk.

"You wanted to see me Sarge?" I said and handed him the note I'd found on my desk.

He paused for a moment, then flicked through the green notebook on his desk, nodding as he did. His lips pursed into a frown and he looked me up and down again. I kept my gaze firmly fixed on the portrait of the Queen that hung on the wall behind his chair and waited for it.

"For starters, it's not 'Sarge', it's Sergeant. I have earned my rank and you will address me as such," he huffed and leaned back in his chair.

"It seems you have a problem with keeping your room in a hygienic state."

This was a trap, and I knew it. It was meant to make me start rambling on about how I thought I had put my PT gear in the wash and that I was sorry about it. But I had been here long enough to know excuses did not work and the outcome was already decided. This was just the precursor to what was to come, and any admission of guilt at this stage would only prolong the ass-kicking. So, I kept silent and braced up.

"Leaving dirty gear in your room will lead to germs being spread amongst your uniforms and possibly end up with you in the RAP (regimental aid post). This would mean you are combat ineffective and of no use to your troops as a leader," he paused for effect, "do you agree?"

"Yes, Sergeant."

"Good, for once we are on the same page. Now, what are we going to do to make sure this doesn't happen again?"

Again, I remained steadfast. I knew he wanted me to start babbling about the fact that I'd learned my lesson and that from now on I'd do all the right things. I also knew he wanted to give me a serve and give me the maximum punishment he could, which in this case, was somewhere between a couple of re-inspections and a day or two of extra duties. Either was fine by me, all I wanted to do was get it over and done with so I could get out of his office.

"Cadet Rickson, you have already been in my office far too many times for someone in 2nd class and I am beginning to think you might not have what it takes to become an officer in this fine Army," he said and stood up from behind his desk.

"I have mentioned this to the OC, and it is clear to both of us that you need to get yourself squared away and quickly," he continued, obviously annoyed at my indignance.

"Are you listening to what I'm saying, Cadet Rickson?"

"Of course, Sergeant. I was just thinking the same," I replied.

In the game of Army discipline, flinching loses every time. Sergeant Zimburger knew this as well I did, but besides the punishments he already had planned, there wasn't much else he could do about it. I could see his temperature rising and knew he would remember this encounter for some time. Bring it on, I thought, I was passing my assessments and wasn't going to start worrying about a few extra's.

"Well, I am glad you are and to help you out, I've penciled you in for two show parades to show us you can keep your PT gear in good nick from here on in," he said and scribbled into his notebook.

"Dismissed Rickson, you can go now," he muttered without looking up.

"Thank you, Sergeant," I said and promptly marched out of his office.

I sauntered back to my room, stopping occasionally for a quick with the handful of cadets who had made themselves comfortable in the company recreation room. I was tempted to head back to my room and put my feet up but figured I might as well grab an early dinner so I could get to work on the tactics papers we'd been issued. Checking my watch, I figured I could beat the rush and get an early dinner, so I continued out of the building and towards the mess. Arriving at the mess, I found the dining room almost empty and belted down a quick feed before jogging back up the steps.

"Rickson, what's your hurry. Don't you know the rules? No running inside the mess," came a shout from the bar.

I knew the voice immediately; cadet Trout was the Long Tan Company Sergeant Major or CSM. As the senior ranking cadet in the company, his role was to lead the company during training activities and ensure the junior cadets maintained their standards. He was also on good terms with their OC and Drilly, so he would have known who was on the shit list and who might need the occasional bit of 'extra training' to bring them up to speed. Although I had heard his voice, I made a quick assessment of the situation and figured I could ignore him and deal with the consequences later. My guess was that he was showing off in front of his friends, because if he had a real reason to pull me up, he would have done it in the lines. The way I looked at it, the extras were all part of the deal and if we couldn't deal with them, we probably weren't cut out to be in the Army. In my head, the only things that mattered were passing tactics, doing well in the field, keeping fit and looking after your mates. I caught up with Watts on the way back to the company.

"Hey mate, how's it hanging?"

"Shit house. PT is killing me, I hate drill and I'm starting to count Mussorians in my sleep," he moaned.

"Cheer up mate, if the PT kills you, you won't have to worry about the Mussorians! As for drill... well, let's face it, everyone hates drill, if you didn't there's something wrong with you," I replied and slapped him on the back.

"Yeah, you're right, I don't think I've got the right body for drill anyway," he said with shrug of his shoulders.

As far as I knew, no cadet in their right mind actually like drill or any sort of parade. This was fine for me, but Watts had the misfortune to be one of the tallest in the company and always ended up as one of the company markers. Markers always stood out on parade and any stuff-ups were in plain sight for everyone watching. Especially Drilly's.

Amongst the rest of my classmate, Watts was somewhat of a rarity, as he was one of the very few cadets in our class that had come straight from high school. The rest of the cadets were either ex-soldiers, had been to university, the Defence Academy, or were on exchange from other countries. For some reason, he had his heart set on joining Armored Corps, which we attributed to the fact that he hated walking but still loved the idea of blowing things up. As a 'tanky' he would be able to do both, as long as he could get through the College first. Luckily for him, he'd ended up in the same section as cadet Walker who was an ex-soldier and ended up spending most of his spare time helping him get organized. Like most of the other ex-soldiers, Walker already had his career planned out after he left the College, which was good for Watts, because besides getting accepted into the Army and wanting to drive a tank, that was about all he had organized.

He wasn't alone though, as I often wondered how I'd ended up at the College. Like plenty of kids in their final year of school, I had plenty of ideas about what I wanted to do, but very little idea about what I was actually going to do. In our final year we were offered a chance to get out and do some work experience to help us make our minds up. I was at a boarding school in regional Queensland, so the opportunities were limited unless you had family or friends with connections in the city. For those of us with nothing else to do, there was a big Air Force base just down the road that was more than happy to take a handful of energetic, albeit confused, teenagers for a week of running around. I figured it would be a good chance to goof-off and possibly meet a few girls from the school up the road. So, with the school counsellor's blessing, off I went.

We spent the week bouncing around various parts of the base, doing a bit of physical training and looking at the occasional plane.

Most of us were knew very little about anything military, with the exception of a couple of students who were Air Force cadets and insisted on pointing out each of the aircraft types while the rest of us did our best to ignore them. Their attempts at being smart were often corrected by the senior non-commissioned officers who were our chaperones and the only thing they convinced me of was that I didn't want to join the Air Force. The only thing that I did enjoy was the day we spent in the base armoury. Having grown up in the country, shooting and fishing were considered mandatory, so the idea of being able to work in a massive gun shop was my idea of heaven. I asked the bloke in the armoury what I'd need to do to be able to get a job there.

"Easy," he replied in between puffs on his cigarette, "Just fuck-up at school like I did."

After asking the Sergeant the same question at the end of the week and found out that I'd need to get good enough marks to get accepted to one of the military trade schools. From there, I'd have to complete basic training, followed by three years of trade training and then I'd be let out in the 'real world'. That made up my mind and I finished the week thinking it hadn't been a total waste of time. Back at school, my friends discussed which university they'd go to and which firm they thought would give them the best start in the corporate world. When someone asked me where I was planning on going, I told them I was joining the military and they looked at me like I was mad. After all, who didn't want a fancy job in some big office in the city? The thought of having to wear a suit and tie every day and grinding away in some glass castle sounded like a shit-house deal to me. I'd rather do something outdoors, especially if it meant the chance to blow some stuff-up while I was at it. At that moment, without realizing it, I has already started to think of myself as a different to my 'civvy' mates and it gave me a sense of purpose that I hadn't had before.

So, I put my head down for the rest of the year to make sure I got the necessary grades. Being a boarder, my fitness was pretty good as I played rugby (anything else was frowned upon), ran cross-country (there wasn't much to do on weekends) and played water-polo (cricket bored the hell out of me). By the time I got the call-up for selection day, I was feeling confident and ready for anything they could throw at me. After a battery of tests, I ended up in front of a young recruiting officer who asked me where I wanted to go. I smiled and said I wanted to work in the armoury. He consulted my grades and asked whether I'd consider trying out for officer training instead. I had no idea what an officer was but figured it would have something to do with guns of some sort and said, why not? That was the last I thought of it. Arriving back home after school finished there was a yellow envelope waiting for me with the Defence Force crest on the top corner. Like the good cadet that I was to become, I duly ignored it and spent the next week celebrating with my mates.

"So, what's next for you then?" my dad asked me over breakfast, as I sat nursing a nasty hangover.

"I joined the Army," I said, nonchalantly.

"What?! When did you do that?" was his startled reply.

"A while ago. I've got to be back by early January to get started."

Being a boarder, I was only ever home on the holidays and usually spent most of my time out of the house getting into trouble with my mates. He was a bit stunned, but like anything else he did, he took it in his stride and nodded. Even though we didn't talk about it much, he'd done a stint in the Army and my grandfather had served in the Pacific in WW2. After a belting New Year's Eve party, I shook off the hangover and jumped on a plane back to Brisbane. At the time, I still had no idea of what I'd signed up for and didn't really care.

Three years later, after scraping through a degree at the Defence Academy and being deemed worthy enough to continue training, I joined my Army classmates as we marched over the hill to the College to finish our training. At the Defence Academy, we trained alongside our peers from the Air Force and Navy, but whilst they left as commissioned officers, we remained cadets (a fact not lost on them). As they set off to their specialist training schools, we joined the cadets who had spent 6 months at the College and would now be our classmates. But how we got there didn't matter once training started. The College didn't care about what school you'd gone to, whether you'd been to university, whether your dad was a General or a bricklayer. It had the same hills for us to run, the same tactics to master and the same obstacles in between. As one of my classmates continually reminded me, 'everyone has got to be somewhere and you're here, so get used to it.'

After we got back to the lines, I grabbed a quick shower and chucked my tactics gear together. A few of us had agreed to meet up in Watts's room after dinner to go over the tactics exercise and prepare our briefs. So, with an armful of pams, maps and notebooks, I made my way up the stairs to Watts's room. As I arrived, I found his door was already open and I could hear the sounds of voices inside.

"Greetings fellow dirtbags," I said and stuck an arm around the door with the middle finger raised.

The voices stopped. I pushed the door open and prepared to chuck my gear onto his bed.

"Ahhh Cadet Rickson, classy as always," said the CSM from his position in the middle of the room.

Watts was standing to attention beside his desk and I could see him stifle a grin as the CSM turned his attention to me. He'd obviously been in the middle of getting a dressing down when I arrived. As I often managed to do, I had achieved the dual outcome of providing my mates with a laugh and getting myself in the shit.

"Good evening CSM," I offered and loosely braced myself up. The relaxed manner in which I attempted the movement failed to impress him.

"Cadet Rickson, you're getting into the habit of being painful, aren't you?" he quipped in response and squared his shoulders towards me.

This was another one of those rhetorical questions that you come to expect from senior cadets. It is always followed by a pause, as they expect you to attempt to explain yourself. As I had already figured the game out, I kept silent and loosened my stance a bit more.

"Now, did I catch you running in the mess earlier this evening?" the CSM continued.

I knew that was going to come back up, although I thought I was at least going to make to tomorrows parade before he caught up with me.

"Wouldn't have been me CSM, I'm not in a hurry when it comes to meals. Bad for your digestion, I'm told," I replied.

I knew that was going to piss him off and saw Watts tighten his lips as he tried not to smile. The CSM, to his credit, remained calm, likely due to the couple of beers he might have put away after dinner. Instead of the usual tongue lashing, he just shook his head and grinned.

"You're already on the Drilly's shit list and now you're on mine. I know you've got a couple of extra duties this week and I'm going to see to it that you end up with more than that. You can kiss your weekends goodbye for the next month."

With that he pushed past me and into the hall. As he pushed past, I sensed him tense up, possibly expecting a bit of resistance and maybe even a bit of a stoush. Instead, I side-stepped him and kicked the door closed as soon as he was outside.

"Fuck mate, you really know how to rub him up the wrong way. You know all of the 1st class are now going to be on your case?" Watts said.

"Fuck 'em if they can't take a joke. They've got 3 months before they graduate, I'll outlast 'em. Remember the motto, *'Illegitimi non carborundum'* - don't let the bastards grind you down," I said and grinned, "Now let's get onto this TEWT otherwise we'll be up all night. Where's Walker?"

"He said he was going to be here, but then again he also mentioned that he might have to drop in to help ... you know who..." he replied, gesturing towards the floor below us.

"Say seen, if seen," I responded.

"Seen!" we yelled in unison.

Our mate Walker was all over the tactics side of training and wasn't afraid to offer his expertise to any of the females who showed him any attention. Before he joined, he's spent a few years working as a barman and was never afraid to ditch his mates when the chance of a bit of female company arose. Which sucked, as we'd have to read and interpret the problem without his help. With his previous experience as a soldier, he was ahead of us when it came to understanding the terrain and enemy tactics. Even though the information we needed was already in our notes, being able to interpret it effectively gave you a much better chance of putting together an effective plan. Whilst there was the occasional cadet who thought they could get away with paying-off any preparations until they got to the exercise area, it was a gamble as the instructors often asked for an initial brief when we arrived. Trying to tap-dance your way through these briefs was a good way to get the instructors offside and certainly guaranteed that your final plan would get plenty of extra attention.

After a couple of minutes reading, we started setting-up our map boards. This fairly rudimentary process was a bit like an artist setting up their easel as it required us to pin our map to a bit of wood (map board) and sticking a bit of clear plastic over the top (talc). The use of the talc allowed you to draw on your map with markers and make changes as the situation changed. This technology was actually the same as we'd be expected to use in the field in real life and in itself was part art, part science. Getting your map board set up wrong automatically drew the attention and ire of the DS, who considered this as bad as not knowing enemy weapon ranges. Mid-way through marking up our boards, someone knocked on the door. We looked at each other, both thinking the same thing.

"Come on in," said Watts.

The door burst open and a sweaty red face stuck around the corner. We both breathed a sigh of relief that it wasn't one of the 1st class.

"Have you blokes done your briefs yet?" Hobbes asked.

"Yeah mate, we're half-way through setting up our talc's," I said.

"Beauty, do you mind if I join you?"

"Come in mate. My house is your house," Watts replied with sweep of his arm.

Hobbes was a pretty relaxed character who lived on the other side of the company. He had the unfortunate luck of being put in a section with a couple of the foreign cadets, who often weren't very interested in doing much preparation for anything. Instead of sitting in his room by himself, he usually ended up joining us and that was fine by us as he was good company.

We spent the next few hours drawing and re-drawing our maps, arguing over which way the enemy would likely come from and drinking instant coffee with stale ration-pack biscuits that Hobbes found in his bag. The clock was closing in on midnight by the time we agreed that we'd done enough. I waved goodbye to my colleagues and stumbled downstairs to my room with my head still spinning with weapon ranges, formations and map coordinates. I collapsed into my 'farter' (bed), only briefly pausing to check my alarm was set before I fell into a deep sleep. Before I joined the military, I had heard stories about soldiers who could fall asleep at the drop of a hat but never believed it. Not anymore. Give me a flat surface and five minutes and I'll show you what sleep looks like.

A Brief Guide to Army Tactics.

Regardless of where you ended up in the Army, soldiers and officers were required to master the basic skills of field combat, which we knew as infantry minor tactics (IMT). These were the core skills of the infantry soldier, which included weapon handling, field craft, defensive and offensive formations. Over the years these basic skills have continued to evolve but will always remain at the heart of everything an Army does. As a cadet these skills were at the heart of everything we did. We learned to 'square away' our weapon-handling and personal gear so we could operate in the field. We did PT to be fit enough to carry a pack and take part in an assault. We learned tactics so we could lead troops on offensive and defensive maneuverers. We learned to look after our mates so they would look after us in battle. No matter what we did, it all came back to being an effective combat soldier first and foremost. Of all these skills, tactics was considered the ultimate military art and failing tactics in any class meant you would not progress. Failure in senior class meant you would not graduate.

...

Friday kicked off at 0530 as my alarm rudely woke me up with a series of loud beeps. I reached up for the switch on the little fluorescent light above the bed and rubbed my eyes. I could have easily stayed in bed for another hour but knew that wasn't going to happen and reluctantly threw my legs over the edge of the bed.

"Here we go again," I said to myself and grabbed a towel off the rack. Like the well-oiled machines we were, it took me under ten minutes to get the three S's done (shit, shower, shave) and be back in my room. I spent the remaining minutes before reveille giving my parade boots another coat of gloss and double checking my uniform.

After roll call, I left my gear laid out on my bed and ran down to the parade ground for daily show parade at 0630.

By itself, a 'showie' was already a pain in the arse, having one on a Friday meant you had to have two uniforms up to inspection standard, as the morning parade was a full march past and dress inspection by the OC. But it was what it was, and after a few months of 'bogging' uniforms, it became second nature. The only advantage to being given a show parade in PT gear was that you could run without being told off for not marching and this gave me a couple of extra precious minutes.

Arriving with a minute to spare, I glanced down the line of 'offenders' to see who else was in the shit this morning. As usual, most of the 'offenders' were 3rd class cadets who were still learning the ropes and had been picked-up by one of the instructors or senior cadets for some minor indiscretion. Occasionally, you'd see a couple of 2nd class who had 'paid-off' their duties or pissed off the Drilly. Very rarely would you see any 1st class, unless they'd managed to really screw up. Today was no different and there were about ten of us on parade, with me as the only 2nd class. I recognized the Duty Officer as one of the cadets from Gallipoli company. He was a tall with a big head and a square jaw who was generally well regarded by the other 2nd class cadets. Rumor had it that he was on someone's shit list and had been made to repeat 1st class due to failing OQ's (officer qualities). Failing OQ's basically meant that your OC didn't think you had the right attitude needed to be an officer. It sounded like bullshit in my books, as I'd read a few military history books and plenty of decorated officers who had gone before us were well known for being less 'polished' than expected. To help with his 'attitude adjustment', it seemed that his OC and/or Drilly had decided the best way to do it was to ensure he ended up with plenty of extra Duty Officer's as well. If you turned up to as many show parades as I did, you got to know which 1st class cadets were on someone's shit list by how many times they pulled

Duty Officer duty. Cadet Woods must have been well into double digits by now, so he was well and truly familiar with routine that we were about to go through. At 0630, he checked his watch one last time and called the parade to attention.

"Righto, you lot, let's get this done. Parade. Atten-shun," he ordered and marched himself into place at the end of the rank.

Whilst his demeanor was serious, his inspections were not as rigorous as we could expect from one of the Drilly's or other senior cadets. He knew what he was looking for, did each inspection efficiently and was straight to the point with his remarks. After all, he'd been in our place not that long ago and knew the game better than any of us. Moving down the line he halted in front of each cadet, checked the 'chit' each carried and did his inspection. Unlike some of his classmates, he showed no particular malice to any of the offenders and simply got on with the job.

"Your collar is good but watch out for starch stains on your sleeves."

"Those toe-caps could do with a bit of work. Give them another coat of gloss when you get the chance."

"Make sure you are careful with the iron, so you don't burn that shirt."

After reminding the cadet next to me to make sure he spent a bit more working on his parade boots, he took a pace forward and halted in front of me. As he turned to face me, I could see him grin and tried to keep a straight face. As my show parade was for the state of my PT uniform, I was the only one in the group not in 'pollies', which meant I stuck out like a sore thumb in my company PT shirt, cap, shorts and runners.

"Ahhh, Rickson, here again I see? Which one of the DS have you managed to piss off this week?"

"Just the Drilly."

"Well, that's not that hard. Did you iron that shirt?" he asked matter-of-factly.

"Yes Corporal, front and back," I replied cynically, before realizing that I should have just said yes and left it at that.

"Well done, smart arse. But let me give you a bit of advice, next time you're on parade and think about saying something funny – don't," he said sternly and shook his head.

With that he snapped his head to the front and continued down the line.

The parade that followed that morning was a relatively straight forward affair. We marched onto the parade ground in company formations, did a bunch of salutes, marched past in quick and slow time, had our uniforms inspected and then marched off again. It was the same week after week, with the only change being which senior officer turned up to review the parade. The Commanding Officer had decided to give the parade a miss this week, so the OC's did the inspections with the CSM and Drilly following along behind them. My rank must have drawn a lucky card as they skimmed through our rank, only stopping at the markers to do a speedy inspection and exchange some brief banter. The rest of the parade went by as expected and before long we were preparing to march off. This wasn't always the case, with some inspecting officers choosing to take their time as they progressed through the ranks. The longer we remained standing, the better the chances that someone would 'bacon' (pass out), so we scanned the ranks around us to look for the tell-tale signs that someone was heading for the pavement. A good 'bacon' would be heard across the parade ground as sound of their rifle clattered against the bitumen. The result would usually be a few extra's and a bit of extra attention from the Drilly next time you were on parade.

Back at the lines, we were given a debrief by the CSM who reminded us about our drill, the standard of our dress and to make sure our salutes were as snappy as possible. These constant reminders were a way of reminding us that someone was always watching, even though most of us developed the habit of keeping straight faced and using the time to think about something else. After being fallen-out, we raced back to our rooms in an organized rabble, knowing we didn't have much time to spare before our next lesson. This time I made sure my drill gear was stashed away neatly, so I avoided any additional punishments that could chew up my leave time over the weekend. The advice from Corporal Woods rang in my ears and I thought I might try to pay back the favor by shouting him a beer if I caught up with him in town over the weekend. I knew Woods was no fan of our CSM the rumor-mill suggested he may have been the cause of the black eye the CSM had been sporting a few weeks ago. This would have also explained all of those extra Duty Officer shifts he had recently pulled. If the big guy thought that the CSM deserved a punch in the nose, I figured we might have at least one thing in common.

After a quick split, we raced over to the lecture halls for rollcall, before we were ushered onto a fleet of buses to head out to the TEWT site. As we bounced along the highway, we discussed the exercise and tried to pick the brains of anyone we thought might have a better solution than ours. The challenge was that most of us had pretty high opinions of ourselves, so it was tough to figure out who knew anything better and who was bluffing. We traded remarks across the aisles while we studied our map boards and argued about the best approach to use. The conscientious ones re-read their pams, recording enemy weapon ranges and formations that might be useful. The lazier ones begged their mates for a copy of their ground brief and furiously scribbled away in their field message notebooks. Each TEWT was a must-pass assessment, so most of us were nervous about the day ahead. In our heads, we mentally rehearsed the ground brief and disposition of the enemy, trying to remember the lessons we had sat though during the previous weeks.

As the bus started to brake, we could see the front gate of the range complex appear. By now Majura had become a 'home away from home' for us as it was the place where we learned the basics of fieldcraft, mastered our weapons and practiced tactical formations. It was home to a number of facilities, including rifle range, training sheds, a tent barracks, mess huts and a couple of thousand acres of hills and valleys. The open slopes of the range were directly in line with the cold winds that blew up from the Brindabella ranges and the snow fields to the south. In winter, the place was cold, dark and usually wet as well. From the end of spring to the middle of autumn, it was still, dusty and stinking hot. The hilly ground was rough and littered with rocks that always managed to find the soft spots on our elbows and knees each time we went to ground. In all, it was a pretty inhospitable place and most of us dreamed of conducting our exercises somewhere where the ground was softer and the temperature much more pleasant.

The buses finally pulled up on the side of the road and we scrambled out to grab our gear from the storage bins. We each lumped our wooden map board under one arm, slung our ech bag over one shoulder and juggled our issued field stool in the other arm. The standard technique for carrying this odd assortment of equipment was to shove the map board into the ech bag and then sling the handles through the fold-up stool. This worked reasonably well for most but there was always an exception to the rule. At least once each TEWT you'd see (or hear) someone try a new technique and see (or hear) it fail spectacularly.

The exercise directing staff (DS) yelled instructions to us as we got off the buses, pointing us towards the designated site for the exercise. As we stumbled up the hill, we joked about which of the DS we would end up with, for as all of us knew, passing TEWTs was due partially to your solution and partially the DS you got. If you were unlucky, you got one of the senior instructors who expected us to know all of enemy weapon types and ranges in detail. If you were lucky, you'd get one of the exchange instructors, who were still learning our tactics and went pretty easy on the cadets in their group. In between lucky and unlucky, lay the rest of the DS, which usually meant you had a decent chance if you'd done your homework.

"Man, I hope I don't get bloody Segurra again," Watts bitched as he puffed his way up the hill.

"Don't stress mate. If you do, just remember he always likes plenty of artillery support and then going in hard and fast," Walker replied.

"What, do you mean there are other options?!" Watts said.

It was a common joke that if you couldn't think of an option, your only choice was 'up the guts with heaps of smoke'. Whilst essentially an old-fashioned approach to warfare, it was still very much a part of Army culture as it instilled in us the necessity of not avoiding a fight, but instead taking the fight directly to the enemy. It was not, however, the correct answer in every situation and DS were often unimpressed by its application, even if they quietly applauded your courage.

At the ridgeline on top of the hill, the lead instructor reminded about the need to work individually with a simple warning for those who thought they could copy other people in the group. Despite all the collaboration beforehand, if you were caught working together on the solution during the exercise, both parties would fail. Each failure would have to be made up out on own time, which usually meant weekends. One of the best ways to piss off the DS was to have them come back and run a re-test on their weekend, so the threat was not taken lightly.

The lead instructor for the TEWT was Captain Lotterman, who was regarded by most of the class as tough but not unreasonable. In Army terms, he was a 'relaxed professional' and carried himself as such. He was well versed in the application of Army tactics and could recite the tech data on every weapons system at ease. In the classroom he delivered lessons in with the usual swagger but wasn't afraid to crack the occasional joke or two to break things up (a rarity among the DS). As he read out the names for each group, we secretly crossed-our fingers and hoped that we would end up with one of the exchange officers. The two exchange officers had gone first, and we could see the relief on the faces of those chosen in their groups. With all but a handful of us left, I heard my name and headed off in Captain Lotterman's direction.

Lotterman had picked a spot under a small gum tree that overlooked the range, and he gathered his group around him to go through the brief one last time. Asking the right question in these settings was a good way of getting yourself off to a good start with the DS. Likewise, asking something really dumb was also a good way to get yourself noticed for all the wrong reasons. Looking around at the group, I saw Davidson and Logan from Alamein, Watts and Hobbes from Long Tan, a couple of blokes from Kokoda and one of the PNG cadets from Gallipoli. In all it looked like a good group, with no 'jack men' who would point out any of your mistakes to the instructor when you presented your solution.

"Righto, does anyone have any questions?" Lotterman asked.

No one was game enough to take a chance this time, so he sent us on our way with a final reminder about staying away from each other and avoiding the 'TEWT farms'. As we scurried off to look for a shady spot to dump our gear, he pulled out a folding chair and propped himself down to observe us as we got to work.

The first thing we had been drilled to do was to check that our location matched what we had marked our maps. Getting your location wrong not only put your solution in doubt, but it also guaranteed that the DS would scrutinize the rest of your plan thoroughly, so it became second nature to check and double-check our location anytime we were on exercise. I looked around to see the rest of the group pouring over their maps, using their compasses to take bearings and re-reading the TEWT papers. I could see Davidson looking puzzled as he shuffled through his notes and scratched his head. He was known for his ability to choose an early night in the farter over a few extra hours of study and I wondered if he might be regretting his choice this time. I tossed a rock in his direction and he looked around as it bounced off a tree in front of him.

"Oi KD, you alright?" I hissed in his direction.

He looked over at Captain Lotterman to check he wasn't looking and shrugged his shoulders.

"Hope so," he mouthed back and grinned.

Captain Lotterman had given us three hours to site a position that would defend the hill against the advancing Mussorian forces. Our final plan would not only have to be marked on our maps, but also laid out on the hill using a handful of wooden 'gun stakes'. As we all had the same bit of ground to defend, it was expected that a few of us would come up with similar plans and this often resulted in clusters of stakes at key bits of the ground. These were the TEWT farms we had been warned about, so we made sure we left a couple of meters between us and the person next to us as we sited each of our positions.

The few hours allotted to the TEWT flew by as I walked and then ran around the perimeter of the position continuously scribbling notes into my small green notebook. I checked and double-checked my gun positions to make sure their fields of fire lined up with what I had drawn on the map. Whilst we were expected to lie down at each position to ensure the fields of fire were accurate, there were always a few cadets who avoided doing so in the hope the DS wouldn't bother to check every position. It was a risk I wasn't going to take for the first exercise, as one poor position would result in the instructor picking apart your plan in front of the group to teach you the importance of 'getting on your guts' when you sited your positions.

I was still the process of putting together my mud model when we heard Lotterman holler, "Righto you lot. That's time. Bring it in here!"

There was always someone who either didn't hear or pretended they hadn't and kept furiously scribbling in their field message notebooks.

"I said now!" Lotterman yelled, his tone making clear that now did in fact mean, now.

We hustled back to where we started, standing in a semi-circle around Lotterman's chair as he sat comfortably.

"Alright, you've got two choices. Either we; (a) work through lunch or, (b) we break for lunch and start in 30 minutes. What's it to be?"

This was never a question, even though it sounded like it might be. The answer was always (a), as we knew that prolonging the inevitable judgement wouldn't change the outcome. The more time you had to sit around and review your solution, the more double guessing you did and the more nervous you felt. He looked around the group, as expected, no one was voting for (b) this time.

"Good, we'll start with the ground and situation brief at..." he looked around at the models we had created, "At Cadet Watt's model, in 2 minutes."

With that we all hustled off to grab our notebooks and headed off in the direction of where Watts had set up. By the looks of it, he had everything done and we ambled over to his position under a wispy tree that overlooked the rolling hills to our south. The lithe branches and sparse leaves of the tree offered some shade, but not quite enough to beat back the heat of the midday sun. His model looked pretty good, with boundaries created out of hootchie cord and the middle filled with various plastic figures marking the key positions. Captain Lotterman surveyed the map with an approving eye and turned to the group.

"Right, who wants to give the ground brief?" he asked, looking around the group.

In theory this was a question, but in practice this was actually the way the DS weeded out who they were going to ask. According to cadet theory, if you looked confident and volunteered, you were unlikely to get picked. Conversely, if you tried to hide up the back, you were almost guaranteed to get picked. The challenge was walking the fine line between looking eager, but not too eager. As I was confident that I'd done enough the night before, I stuck my hand up and volunteered. Being our first TEWT, I thought I might as well get it out of the way, and even better, it might buy me a few points with Captain Lotterman.

"Cadet Rickson, you think you've got this?" Lotterman asked.

"Yes Sir, I think I do," I replied politely.

"Good, in which case we might have a look at it later. In the meantime, Cadet Davidson, you can do the ground brief for us."

Watts looked at me and grinned. We both knew that there was a better than average chance that he hadn't done one last night, but he could 'tap dance' pretty well when put on the spot.

"Yes Sir," replied KD snappily and started flipping through his notebook.

Whilst the ground brief wasn't a pass or fail component of the TEWT, it was a good way for Captain Lotterman to check on how much preparation we'd done. A poorly put together, or non-existent ground brief was guaranteed to put the instructor offside and ensure your final plan was scrutinized in detail. As importantly, it was likely to lead to a badly constructed tactical plan, which was rammed home to us time and time again. Like everything else we did, there was a balancing act in trying to decide how much time we'd spend on doing something that wasn't a pass or fail requirement instead of preparing uniforms, doing other homework or sleeping.

KD started his brief confidently, getting the basic background information and details about the terrain mostly right. At some stage into the enemy forces brief, he started to stumble, and I glanced sideways at Captain Lotterman, expecting him to cut him off. Instead, he let KD bumble his way through the rest of it.

"And that concludes the brief, any questions?" KD concluded and looked around the group.

The group looked around sheepishly as we wracked our brains to come up with a question that he could answer correctly.

"Stop there, Cadet Davidson," Lotterman said slowly.

"You either did not read the TEWT papers or have paid off doing any work on it. Not only have you got the enemy forces wrong, but you have also recorded our position as..." he paused to consult his notes before pointing to the top of the ridge, "About half a kilometer away from where we are. Come see me after we're finished."

"Yes Sir," KD replied and skulked back into the ranks.

"Alright Rickson, you can fill us in with the details that were missed. Please do not screw this up," Captain Lotterman said as he scribbled into his notebook.

Thanks to our late-night efforts, I managed to get the rest of the details mostly correct. Captain Lotterman nodded and checked his watch, indicating that I'd done a passable job. The next step in the process was the presentation of each lot of battle orders and a review of each of our positions on the ground. We made our way to each of the models and listened to the owners as they read their orders to the group. Most of the models were pretty similar, being made up of varying types of string, plastic army figures and assorted toothpicks or cocktail stirrers. On the odd occasion, Captain Lotterman would raise an eyebrow when he saw something out of the ordinary. In our case, we could see Lotterman shaking his head as we turned up at Logan's model. The string was there, as were the little green army men and cocktail flags.

"And what exactly are these supposed to represent?" Lotterman asked in a slow drawl, motioning towards the small piles of dry kangaroo poo that were assembled around the map.

"These are the known enemy locations, Sir."

Lotterman shook his head and the rest of us stifled a laugh.

"Adapt, improvise and overcome Sir," Logan said with a grin.

After listening to Logan's orders, we walked around the perimeter and checked the positioning of each gun pit. Any position that was located in one of the TEWT farms, resulted in Lotterman calling out those responsible and getting them onto the ground to demonstrate exactly why they had chosen the position. This often resulted in more laughs as they tried to tap-dance their way through their explanations. Where we could, we'd chip in with questions to try to help our colleagues look like they'd done the work, but Lotterman knew exactly what we were up to and pulled us up quickly where it was evident that the position was unworkable. After an hour of kneeling or lying down at each position and explaining our plans, our brains were fried by the continuous barrage of GPS co-ordinates, weapons ranges, expected enemy movements and acronyms. On return to the ridge, Lotterman collected our written orders and sent us on our way. Our results would be posted later in the week once they had been reviewed to check for any plans that might be a bit too similar.

Looking around at my classmates as we boarded the buses to return, they looked spent but happy. We'd jumped through one more hurdle and most were confident that they'd scraped through. On the bus ride back to the College, we shared stories about the public arse kicking's that had taken place during the day and did our best to commiserate with those that had received them. We knew we still had plenty to learn but felt like we'd taken an important step towards becoming the tactical gurus we were expected to be as junior officers.

With the first TEWT complete, the next step would be to put these lessons into practice in the field. We spent the next few weeks in barracks being drilled in the conduct of platoon operations and how manage our troops on the battlefield. The field instructors taught us the art of reconnaissance, how to develop a quick attack plan and the most effective way to deploy our sections during an attack. In the evenings, we packed and repacked our field gear. We arranged and re-arranged the pouches on our packs and webbing, always looking for a better way to stash things so they were at our fingertips when we needed them. As we'd learned from our initial field training, most of our issued field kit was bulky and next to useless when it was cold and wet. It didn't matter how tough you were, walking around in woolen jumpers with plastic raincoats didn't make for much fun. Or decent sleep. Even though we had issued lists that told us what equipment we were supposed to pack for the field, anyone with half a brain replaced as much of it as they thought they could get away with.

All of us wished we could replace our issued boots, which filled up with water and did nothing to keep you warm. However, without a 'chit' from a doctor, you couldn't replace them. Anything you wore on a daily basis that could be seen, such as your fatigues, was also out. If it wasn't Army disruptive pattern camouflage uniform (DPCU) it would stand out and get pinched by the DS. So, we focused on anything that would keep us warm, dry or make it easier to heat up a brew faster. We searched local army disposal stores, hiking shops and mail catalogues to find the lightest, warmest and most durable gear that came in camouflage, olive green or black. We debated the merits of down vs polar-fleece jumpers, whether Gore-Tex gloves were worth it, and which sleeping bags were the lightest. Pretty fast even the most conscientious among us became 'bongo kings' and happily replaced anything they thought would make life easier in the field. The one catch was, you couldn't get caught with it, as the field staff were pretty strict when it came to non-issued gear. If they caught you with it, it was likely to be confiscated. If that meant you didn't have a jumper, then so be it. Like many things at the College, it was a lottery, but if it meant being warm and dry, we figured it was worth rolling the dice.

Each company had their own resident bongo king, and in Long Tan we had Walker. As an ex-digger with plenty of bush time, he had brought a heap of his non-issued gear with him. He helped us find lighter, warmer synthetic sleeping bags, wind-stopping polar fleece and thermal underwear that we could hide under our fatigues. With his guidance, we reconfigured our packs, so we didn't have to go digging through our gear when we needed things and made sure our straps didn't continuously dig into our shoulders.

"Jesus, Watts! What the fuck have you got in this bloody thing?!" he asked when he saw Watts's pack during one of our late-night field preparation sessions.

"Everything on the field list. I think," Watts replied as his pack hit the ground with a thump.

"And one of everything from the 'gumpy' machine downstairs too!" I chimed in.

"Piss off. Ok, ok, there might be a few jack rats (rations) in there as well," he grinned.

Walker had his work out cut out for him to get Watts's gear into field shape, but he loved this stuff and his hands worked in machinelike fashion as he pulled the pack apart and steadily rebuilt it again. The rest of us watched on and adjusted our own gear, checking pouches, tightening straps and wrapping up loose ends in hundred mile-an-hour tape.

A week before we were due to depart, the platoon and section lists were posted on the company notice boards. We checked the lists as soon as they went up and crossed our fingers that we would end up with a few mates in our section. We also checked to see which DS we'd have, as this was often a big part of whether we'd pass or fail. With a couple of days to go, we'd get together with our section mates to split up ration-packs and do deals with our section mates as to what stores we would end up with. Radio batteries were always a pain in the arse, as were the training rocket launchers, or 66's as we knew them. The batteries were like bricks and each section would have to hump a few of them, as the old radio's chewed through them at a rapid rate, especially when it was cold and wet. The 66's were also a pain, as you had to carry them slung around your shoulder, just in case you needed one in an attack. They were on flimsy slings and the ends had the unnerving capability to find the back of your head every time you dived for cover. But there was no way to avoid them, so we did deals with our section mates and did our best to cram whatever we ended up with in our packs.

With the sky turning grey above us on Monday morning, we humped our loaded packs down to Field Training Wing to meet up with our sections and wait for the trucks to turn up. I dumped my gear on the grass next to the rest of the section.

"Reckon we might be in for a bit of rain this week?" Hobbes asked, as he lay back on his pack.

Next to him sat Bensonhurst, who stroked his chin and replied, "If it ain't rainin', it ain't trainin'."

"Yeah, that would be right. The field training stuff must order it with the field stores," Hobbes said with a shake of his head.

The rest of us agreed that it probably would and resigned ourselves to the fact that we'd be spending another week in the field humping around in wet gear. Somehow, each time we were due to go on exercise, the weather would manage to turn stinking hot and dusty, or raining sideways and freezing cold.

"Does anyone know exactly where we're going?" a voice behind me asked.

It was EJ, one of the girls from Kapyong. Even though she was tiny and seemed to disappear under her pack, she seemed to enjoy field exercises.

"South coast somewhere," I replied.

"I heard one of the field DS talking about it getting pretty cold up in the hills and saying something about it being a long week. Do you think this might be the start of exercise Timor?" she asked, and we all turned around to look in her direction.

"I bloody hope not, I missed breakfast this morning!" Bensonhurst responded.

Whilst everything up to now had made sense, maybe the DS might be planning something sneaky. We'd heard rumors about exercise Timor and knew it was coming at some stage. Exercise Timor was designed as a test of our leadership abilities but wasn't on any of the class programs. It meant going without sleep and food for a few days, maybe a week, as were put through our paces in various field situations. None of us really had any idea of when it would occur or where it would be held as it was kept a secret by the DS and the cadets who had already been through it. Each time we started preparing to go field, the threat lurked in the back of our minds. In my head, I went through all the gear that I'd packed to make sure I was as prepared as I could be for a week of being cold, wet, hungry and tired. Luckily, I didn't have too much time to think about it as the trucks started to roll-up.

"Righto, you lot. Load up," boomed a voice from behind us.

We looked at each other and shrugged.

"Driver, drop me at the pub. I'll practice my offensive operations there," I said as I hauled myself into the back of the truck.

"You're not wrong, your activities at The Moose are generally pretty offensive," EJ added, which raised a few laughs from the rest of the section.

"Offensive, yes. But on occasion, I have been known to be victorious," I replied with a wink.

"Very, very, very rarely," Troy added dryly from behind me and shook his head.

Once we were all inside the canvas backed trucks, we heard the starter motors squeal as the convoy started up. The convoy crawled through the barracks and out the front gates. The trucks swayed through the turns as we headed for the highway. We listened as the engines whined before settling into the steady hum of their highway rhythm. We tried peeking out of the tightly laced tarp sides but couldn't make out anything more than the open spaces of the country as we barreled down the road. For the next couple of hours, the trucks ground along the freeway, slowing occasionally as we went through small towns and intersections. Eventually, we slowed to a crawl and we heard the tires grip onto the dirt. Wisps of dust and the smell of eucalyptus crept in through the sides of the tarps as we wound along a series of back roads. Finally, the convoy shuddered to a halt and the engines died. We heard feet hit the ground outside the truck moments before the tarp on the back was thrown up.

"Ok, you lot. Out you get!" the driver ordered.

Poking my head out from the canvas, I saw nothing but dense scrub surrounding us. As we hauled our gear off the truck, I could hear the DS calling for their sections. We'd drawn Sergeant Dawson, who scowled at us from the side of the road as he called the roll. His face was chiseled into permanent frown lines and it looked like it might crack if he ever tried to smile. We were the first section in the platoon, and I looked down the road to see the other two sections going through the same routine. Looking down the road, I could see Sergeant Ruth and Warrant Officer Rogers in front of the other sections. Even though Ruth was in drill wing, we could tell that he would rather be out in the field. Try as he might, he was not put together to be on a parade ground and you could see he was a lot more relaxed when he was in the field. Rogers was the senior field instructor and was well respected amongst staff and cadets alike. He had spent most of his career in the infantry, so the College was likely to be a rest posting for him. Like Ruth, he was more at home in the field than he was in the barracks and you could see him smile when he looked out into the scrub from where he stood. The only other time we'd seen him smile was on the rugby paddock, where he toiled away in the scrum and was known for his willingness to settle up scores at the bottom of a ruck.

"Platoon commander!!" yelled Captain Yeoman from a small clearing off the side of the road.

"Yes, sir!!" came a voice from one of the other sections.

"Get over here!"

Our first platoon commander hustled down the road with his webbing flapping around him. For each of the exercises we'd do from now on, each platoon would also have one of the tactics instructors accompanying them. Along with being assessed as section commanders, we would also be assessed as platoon commanders to see if we could put in practice what we'd learned in the classroom. Over the course of the next week or so, we'd rotate through platoon headquarters, filling each of the roles in the command group and being put through our paces as platoon commanders. Just like our tactics lessons, field assessments were must pass and any failures would result in retests. As the platoon would be operating on its own, the platoon commander was on their own when it came to tactical decision making, which could be daunting with the DS standing behind you at all times. Luckily, the section commanders were able to assist when it came to planning attacks and setting up positions. Like everything else we did, we relied on our mates to get us through and this was never as important as when we were being assessed as platoon commanders. As novice field tacticians, we had plenty to learn and knew that our chances of passing were a lot better if our section commanders helped out.

The rest of us sat on our packs as we waited for the new platoon commander, or 'balloon commander', to receive his orders from Captain Yeoman. We knew that the first job of the platoon commander would be to locate our exact position on the map before he could give his initial set of orders. Even though we had been reminded continuously about the importance of knowing exactly where we were, map reading is as much of an art as it is a science, and there were always a couple of cadets who didn't quite get it. Once we were away from the classroom, the numerous contour lines began to blend into each other and the main features were easily hidden by the dense scrub, making it difficult to find the elusive 'eight figure grid reference' that we were expected to produce at a moment's notice.

Through the eucalypts I could see our platoon commander fiddling around with his map and compass, taking the occasional look around before placing a finger on the map. From where we were, I couldn't hear Captain Yeoman's exact reply, but it was pretty clear that it wasn't the right answer.

The Balloon Commander Joke

During WW1, a young officer was out flying reconnaissance in his balloon when he became temporarily 'disorientated', so he brought the balloon down and found a man on a horse.
"Excuse me," he asked the man, "Do you mind telling me where we are?"
The man looked at up him and then at the countryside around him.
"Yes, Sir. You are in the middle of a field, twenty feet in the air and suspended below a large cloud of hot air," he replied The Balloon Commander nodded and replied, "Thank you Private, but how did you know I was an officer?
The man grinned and said, "Because Sir, you are twenty feet in the air, suspended below a large cloud of hot air and have no idea where you are. How did you know I was a Private?"
"Easy young man," the officer replied with a smile, "What you told me was 100% correct, but totally bloody useless."

...

Captain Yeoman was from the infantry and he took his job very, very seriously. He was particularly passionate about battlefield tactics and was one of the very few officers we had on staff who had been on the operations. Amongst the cadets he was known as 'the killer of men' as he had the look of a man who wouldn't be afraid to slit your throat while you slept, so we didn't stuff around when he was in charge.

After a few more minutes, the platoon commander must have got our position correct and he called the section commanders in for the first set of orders. The rest of us hunkered down on our packs and double-checked our gear. I'd drawn the number two spot to the section gunner and would be sharing a hootchie with one of the blokes from Alamein that we called Dig.

"Have we got time for a brew? What do you reckon?" he said as he sprawled back over his pack.

"Dunno, maybe," I replied and handed him one of the half-crushed biscuits that I'd fished out of my webbing.

"Hey Sarge, have we got time for a brew?" he asked in the direction of Sergeant Dawson.

Dawson looked over at the clearing and then at his watch.

"If you can get one finished in under five minutes, I reckon you do."

In my head I did the math; thirty seconds to get my brew gear out, a minute to boil water and another fifteen seconds to stir in the ingredients. That left just over a minute to belt it down, with the likelihood of burning the hell out of my mouth in the process. Achievable, but I had burned the top layer of skin off the roof of my mouth one too many times.

"A smoke it is then," Dig said, having come to the same conclusion I had.

He rustled around in his webbing and produced a pack of rolling tobacco, which he threw my way.

"Here, roll one of these for us."

I shook my head, amazed at his capacity to be both efficient and lazy at the same time. There was a handful in each company who were dedicated smokers in the barracks, but for some mysterious reason that number doubled when we were in the field. I had become a field smoker during one of our first exercises and had almost mastered the art of rolling the dodgy looking cigarettes we referred to as 'bush darts'. Get it right and it would light and smoke quickly during one of the many quick breaks we'd get each day. Stuff it up, and the thing would fall apart in your hands, much to the amusement of whoever was around you. I was half-way through finishing when I saw our section commander come running back down the road.

"Save it for later Dig, looks like we're on the move," I said and threw everything back into the pouch.

The Possum had drawn first shift as 'seco' and was sweating up a storm by the time he got back from getting his initial brief. Out of the corner of my eye, I saw Sergeant Dawson look up from where he sat on his pack.

"Righto guys," he puffed, "bring it in."

He laid out his map and pointed to it as he talked. We looked at it briefly but didn't pay much attention as we knew the only person in the section that had to know this was the section 2IC (second in command).

"Our first objective is to clear all the way to the high ground to our south," he said and gestured towards the bush on the opposite side of the road.

"Time is now... 1307, moving in five minutes. All weapons to action from here. Guns on the right, scout stick around for a bearing."

With that, we hustled back to our packs and threw them over our shoulders. The metal-on-metal of our weapons being cocked echoed through the trees as we checked our pouches were closed and adjusted the straps on our packs. From here on in, our days would be spent communicating in whispers and hand-signals only. Looking over at Poss, he gave us the 'get up and go' signal and the section got to its feet to start the patrol.

As it had been a while since we'd been in the field, our patrolling skills were rusty, and the sounds of snapping branches and heavy footfalls in the undergrowth could heard through the trees. The DS walked around the sections, reminding us to watch where we put our feet and to keep our positions in the formation. Occasionally, you could hear them providing a bit of guidance through the trees.

"Oi, you two! Are you rooting?! Get away from each other and spread the fuck out!"

"That way fuck-knuckle! Point your rifle where you are looking."

"Hey dopey, stop looking at your feet and look where you are going!"

Each time we heard the DS yell, Dig and I would grin and check to make sure we weren't doing the same thing.

Our first contact came late in the afternoon as we made our way through a dry riverbed. I heard the first couple of shots and looked at Dig. He looked around and shrugged.

"Are they shooting at us?" I whispered and looked towards where the Possum and Sergeant Dawson were.

The Possum looked confused and started pulling his map out.

"What the fuck are you doing section commander?" Dawson said, resting his weight on the stick he carried in place of a rifle. The Possum looked around again and raised his rifle.

"Scouts?" he called.

"Contact front!!!" came the reply from one of the scouts.

Dawson shook his head and turned to the section.

"Contact fucking front! Get on your guts! Section commander, get control of your section."

More shots rang out from the high ground ahead of us. The distinct metallic sound of our enemies' rifles could be clearly heard through the trees. I hit the ground and crawled forward to where Dig was lying. We could hear the section radio start to crackle as the signaler called the contact in.

"Target location?" Possum called to the scouts.

"Approximately one hundred meters straight ahead, two enemy behind a dead tree," came EJ's high pitched response.

"Get that fucking gun going!" Dawson yelled and pointed in our direction.

Dig didn't need any further encouragement and he swiveled the gun around in the enemy direction. I heard the 'click' of the safety switch just before the gun barked to life and started to throw brass into the foliage beside him.

"Can you see 'em?" I asked, squinting through the dense scrub.

"Not a chance," he replied with a grin and squeezed the trigger again.

Behind us the rest of the platoon grouped together and started to get into formation for an attack. As we'd managed to 'find' the enemy first, our section provided covering fire for the rest of the sections put in an attack from a flanking position. The ensuing battle took the better part of half an hour and was not without plenty of hiccups. With plenty of guidance from the DS, we managed to take out a couple of scouts from the Mussorian 101st regiment who had been camped out on a small rise.

"Righto, you lot. Leave your packs where they are and get in here!" Yeoman yelled from a spot in the clearing where the enemy lay.

The next twenty minutes was spent on a debrief, which included a cameo from the dead enemy. Each of the DS ran through the parts of the contact that they had witnessed and pointed out all of the mistakes we had made. Nothing escaped their sharp eyes and they picked holes in our firing positions, how we worked as teams and the way we conducted the attack. We chuckled at each other's screw ups and made mental notes of what we'd do differently next time. The Possum got his fair share of attention and by the end of it, you could see his cheeks glow red under his sweat stained camouflage cream. He wasn't alone and we all got a mention of some sort. Dig and I copped a flogging for where we'd positioned the gun, even though we thought we'd managed to hide from Dawson's view. We should have known better as it turned out that Dawson had been watching us the whole time. By the end of the debrief, we'd reset ourselves from 'barracks mode' to 'field mode' and you could see everyone sharpen up as they moved silently back to their packs.

Another hour or so later, we found ourselves halted at the base of a small hill that was covered in light brush and bracken. Checking my watch, I held my extended arm up to the horizon and tried to judge when sunset would be. Couldn't be more than two or three fingers before it hit the horizon, I thought.

"What do you reckon Dig, this'll be it for the night?" I whispered and rolled onto my side.

We had been stopped up for a few minutes now and I'd just seen Possum race off in the direction of the platoon commander.

"Hope so, I've had enough walking for the day," he replied and rested his head against the side of the gun.

I looked over towards the section signaler, Heather, who was slumped against a tree with the radio handset tucked under her ear.

"Pssst," I called over to her and raised myself up on one elbow.

She looked over and I held up both hands in the cadet field signal for 'what's going on?'. She looked towards Sergeant Dawson before looking back my way. She joined her index finger and thumb together into a circle and put it on her nose, 'fuck nose. I grinned and gave her a thumbs up.

"She says she doesn't know," I said in a low.

Beside me, Dig fumbled in his pouches and found a block of ration pack chocolate. Around us the bush was eerily quiet, the silence broken by an occasional bird call or the rustle of a cadet trying to get comfortable on the dry leaves. I was almost dozing off when the Possum came bustling back through the scrub and gave us the field signal to get moving again. I'd been right, the high ground above us was going to be our harbor for the night. Before moving into our night position, we patrolled around the base of the hill, scouting for possible avenues the enemy could use to sneak up on us at night and finding the best spots for our guns. Even though we followed field protocols to the letter, somehow the Mussorian patrols managed to find us most nights. We knew that at some stage we'd be forced out of our sleeping bags by the unmistakable sound of shots, so we focused on finding the most comfortable bits of ground to set up our hootchies and hoped that any probes would be done after we'd got a few hours of shut eye.

With half an hour before last light, the platoon commander walked the perimeter for the final time, checking each of the gun positions and making sure the sections had set out their defenses properly. The platoon commander was a bloke from Alamein company who we called Chuck, and he had Captain Yeoman in tow as he followed the perimeter cord around the position.

"Dig, the DS is coming. Make sure your bloody eyes are open," I hissed as I saw them approach our position.

From my position to the side of the gun, I couldn't see whether he was awake or not. After a sold day of patrolling, there was a chance that he might be 'relaxing' his eyes as he lay behind the gun. Getting caught napping on the gun was a sure-fire way to get a decent arse-kicking from the DS and end up on their shit list for the rest of the exercise.

"Piss off, I'm awake," he replied and lifted his head slightly.

We heard footsteps approaching our position as Chuck walked towards us. Captain Yeoman had stopped to chat with Sergeant Dawson in the center of our section position.

"G'day lads, how's it going?" Chuck whispered as crouched down beside us.

"All good mate. How's the balloon commanding going?" Dig replied.

"Not bad, but I'll be glad to get back to the section tomorrow. You blokes got any flares out front?" he asked.

"Yeah, I put one down in the dead ground about fifty meters to our half left. What time do you reckon the fun will kick off tonight?" I said and motioned in the direction of the dead ground.

"No idea. Yeoman keeps his cards pretty close to his chest. Knowing him, I'd say it would be right in the middle of the night though."

"That'll screw our beauty sleep right up. And god knows, Dig needs as much as he can get," I replied.

"Piss off, you're no oil painting either!" he fired back.

I gave him the finger and we all chuckled quietly.

"Righto, I'm off then. Have a good one," Chuck said and headed back off in the direction of platoon headquarters.

A couple of minutes later, we heard the Possum sneak up behind us.

"Stand-to," he whispered and then made his way around to the next pit.

The sun had disappeared over the horizon and the last rays of light turned the sky pink overhead. Out front, the platoon clearing patrol was circling our position, arming the flares we'd set and looking for any signs of the enemy. The rest of the platoon 'stood-to' from their positions, lying at the ready just in case the enemy attempted to sneak up on us. Even though this routine seemed out of place in a world of high-tech night vision and thermal imaging, it was an important part of training and we knew better than to argue with the instructors. I didn't mind as I had grown to love this time of the day, watching the colors slowly fade and listening to the sounds of the bush as the day critters handed over to the night ones. As the color drained out of the sky, birds found their night perches and the various types of ants slowly scampered back to their holes. The greens slowly became greys as the trees around us blended into blurry shapes and we were left in silence.

"Stand-down," whispered our section 2IC from behind us.

"About bloody time," Dig replied and rolled over onto his back.

"You blokes know what picket you're on?" Logan asked as he plonked himself down beside him.

"Dig's first and I've got the split," I answered and handed him the luke-warm brew that had been sitting beside the gun.

"Ahh, sweet and hot, just like me," Logan said as he took a sip.

"And yet, unlike any of your women," Dig replied.

Logan lifted his hand with two fingers raised and grinned.

"Alright then you blokes, I'll see you in the morning," he announced and got up to leave.

For the next three quarters of an hour, Dig and I lay motionless as we waited for our shift to finish. We talked in whispers as we swapped ration pack biscuits and the last of the cold coffee. As the temperature started to drop, we shivered and hoped for the time to pass a bit quicker so we could head off to the warmth of our sleeping bags. Eventually, I heard the rustling of footsteps along the path and I was relieved when EJ turned up to replace me.

"All yours EJ, enjoy and don't let Dig go to sleep. His snoring will wake up the entire Mussorian regiment," I whispered as I got up.

"I can't promise anything but I'm guessing that they'll find us anyway," she replied.

I followed the perimeter chord that ran back to where we'd set up our hootchie, doing my best not to make too much noise in the dark. Somehow, we'd managed to find a reasonably flat spot between two saplings that was just big enough to fit the two of us. The ground was hard and hid a number of rocks beneath the dry leaves, but at least we wouldn't have to prop ourselves against our packs to stop rolling down the hill. Added to that, I could see a full blanket of stars above us, which meant rain was unlikely. I picked the hootchie off the ground and secured both ends to trees before slipping my boots off and crawling into my sleeping bag. I adjusted my webbing under my head and made sure my rifle was tucked in under the side of my sleeping bag before closing my eyes.

"Bloody luxury," I chuckled and was asleep minutes later.

I was woken by the sounds of rifle shots ringing out through the trees. I was warm in my sleeping bag and could feel the cold air on my face. *Maybe, they'll just go away*, my sleep addled brain thought. Dig was still snoring beside me and for a moment, I thought it might just happen. Unlikely.

"Stand-to you lot," someone hissed from the gun pit.

"Roger. Dig, get up," I replied and gave him a nudge.

"What... Fuck off. It's not my turn ... Fuck off," he grumbled and rolled over.

I steeled myself against the cold and slid out of my sleeping bag. "Get up boof-head, we're getting probed," I said as I pulled my boots on and slid my webbing over my shoulders.

"Fuck off. Not my turn. I'm not going. Ya can't make me," he replied and begrudgingly unzipped his sleeping bag.

I reached up for the perimeter cord and shuffled over to the gun pit.

"Who's that?" Heather said from behind the gun.

"Just me, where's the bad guys?"

"Around to our left somewhere I think," Troy said from his position beside Heather.

We sat in silence and listened for any signs of movement. After a few minutes, Dig shuffled in beside us and was still pulling his boots on when the first flare went up.

"Well, there goes the neighborhood," Troy said and ducked down to avoid the strobing light that reached through the trees.

One of the pits to our right opened up with a series of single shots, followed moments later by a volley of returned fire from the enemy at the bottom of the hill. We heard the sounds of hurried footsteps through the bush as the section commander raced between positions. In the distance, I thought I could hear a rifle being cocked and searched the darkness for signs of moment. Nothing. We sat in silence. Eventually the Possum tripped and stumbled his way over to us. The DS had decided that we'd done our bit to defend ourselves for the night and we could return to the warmth of our farters again.

"Any bets that isn't the last of it?" Heather asked, always the pessimist.

"Even money, I reckon," Dig replied.

The two of us shuffled back to our hootchie and slid into our cold sleeping bags. Knowing Yeoman, we thought it was a better than average chance that there would be at least a couple of probes each night, so we left our boots on and made sure our packs were close by before zipping ourselves back into our sleeping bags.

I had only just settled into a deep sleep when I was woken by someone outside the hootchie giving me a gentle nudge.

"What do you want? Who is it?" I hissed.

"You're up for picket mate, get out of bed," Logan said from a crouch beside me.

I rubbed my bleary eyes as my addled brain tried to figure out what had happened.

"Are you sure?" I whispered.

"Of course, I'm sure. Would I lie to you?" he replied.

"It's been known to happen," I said and started to unzip my sleeping bag.

The sound of the zipper was all he needed, and I heard his muffled footsteps head back in the direction of his hootchie as I pulled myself out of my sleeping bag. The few hours of broken sleep I'd managed to get had only left me feeling tired and I had to drag myself over to the gun pit. Hobbes was lying back on his webbing when I got there.

"Ahh, waiter. I will have coffee, bacon and eggs, and a copy of today's Telegraph," he whispered as I sat beside him.

"You're shit out of luck mate. The kitchen is closed until lunch and all we've got 'til then is tinned cheese and biscuits," I replied.

"In which case, I'll take the biscuits, but you can keep the cheese. That stuff is no good for you," he shot back.

In the twilight, I could make out the whites of his teeth as he grinned back at me. For the next half an hour we sat in the darkness and waited for the first glimpses of daylight to appear. Just before stand-to, Hobbes went around and kicked the rest of the section out of their beds. In the bush around me, I could hear the platoon wrestling with their sleeping bags, fumbling around for boots and zipping up their jackets. In the silence of the early dawn, each little sound seemed to be amplified and I realized why the instructors put so much effort into our basic field skills.

Little by little, the daylight started to creep over the horizon. The leaves went from tangled, dark shapes to hazy grey and then finally, sharp green. It was as if someone had turned the color back on again. Around us, the ants crawled out of the ground and as the light returned, I found a large grasshopper happily sitting on top of the gun, looking at us intently. The clearing patrol went around our position with Sergeant Dawson following them stealthily. When the DS were happy that we'd secured the perimeter again, we stood down and got started for the new day.

The start of each day meant we'd be changing positions as we rotated through each of the roles within the platoon. As number two on the gun yesterday, the new day brought about a 'promotion' to number 1 on the gun. So, I bid Dig farewell as we packed up our sleeping gear and welcomed Hobbes as my offsider.

"How we goin' with them bacon and eggs chef?" he asked as he tossed his pack down next to mine.

"Well, I'm afraid I've got bad news for you mate. The egg delivery was cancelled due to the chickens going on strike and the bacon plane was held up in customs. But the good news is, if you like terrible coffee, we've got heaps of it," I replied.

The flame on the gas burner glowed blue under the steel cups-canteen that was perched over it. As the water bubbled away, a tin of baked beans was slowly warming up in the canteen and the makings of a coffee waiting on the ground beside it. Working together, we took turns behind the gun to conduct our daily routines. This started by boiling up a mug of water while I cleaned the gun, brushed my teeth and chewed on a muesli bar. With the water boiled, I'd pour some of it into a small plastic tub that had my razor in it. The rest of the water was made into muddy coffee, which I shared with Hobbes, whilst I attempted to shave. Removing the mixture of sweat, dirt and camouflage cream that built up on your face in the field was no simple task. The issued cam-cream was sticky stuff and it clogged up your razors pretty quick if you didn't scrub it off before shaving. As a result, most of the blokes grew dodgy looking moustaches in the field as it meant one less bit of cam-cream to remove. The whole procedure would take a well drilled cadet about ten minutes and could be done in less if you were game enough to attempt a dry shave. This was akin to licking a strip of sandpaper and was generally avoided at all costs. By the time we were done changing positions, finishing our morning routines and rotating the various stores amongst the section, we were ready to go again. With EJ slotting into Possum's vacated section commander spot, she wandered around to each of the pits to give us an update.

"So, boys, are you ready for the good news?" she said as she knelt beside us.

"There's good news?! This is new," Hobbes said with a smile.

"Well, there's no bad news yet, but give it time and it will happen," I chimed in.

"The good news is that we get to patrol the area to the south today, seeking out, closing with, capturing or killing any of the Mussorians we find. Doesn't that sound like fun?" EJ chirped.

"Well, I don't have anything better to do today. Hobbes, how's your schedule looking?"

"I'd have to check with my secretary, but I think I'm free. I do have one request though."

"Don't tell me," EJ said and looked thoughtful for a second, "No hills..."

"Or rocky spots. Or leeches. Or anything unpleasant really. And next time we find the enemy, can you make sure it is on a nice soft bit of grass or possibly light sand as I've recently come up with an allergy to rocks and hard stuff."

"I'll see what I can do. Have a good day fella's," she said, smiled and headed off to the next pit.

"Why is she always so fucking happy?" Hobbes said in disgust.

I put my index and thumb together and placed it over my nose.

The rest of the day followed the same routine as the day before. Patrol for an hour or so, cross a few obstacles, find the enemy, battle our way to them, debrief and then do it all over again. Sometimes we'd get bumped early in the morning, sometimes later, but always once before lunch. Then we'd find a spot to harbor up so the 2IC's could check our rations and ammunition. This usually occurred in the vicinity of the porta-loos that seemed to follow us around on our exercises and provide a place to top up our water bottles and dump our rubbish. After a while, we got pretty good at guessing where they would be located and would try to figure out how close the next enemy position was based on when we had seen the last port-a-loos.

We humped up scrubby hillsides, through dense brushlands, over dry riverbeds and swampy valleys. No matter where we went, we'd manage to find a handful of Mussorians hiding on top of a hill or convenient bit of high ground. By day three, our barracks habits had worn away and the platoon had slipped into a steady rhythm. The first shots would ring out and the platoon would hit the deck as one.

"Contact front!" the lead section would yell in unison.

The gunners would find what high ground they could (without being reminded by their DS) and the tail-end Charlies would close up to the back of the section. Section commanders and the platoon commander would run through a quick reconnaissance before drawing up a plan for the attack. One section would inevitably hold fast as fire support, with another assaulting from one of the flanks and the third in reserve behind them. By the end of the week, we thought we were getting pretty slick and were almost up to the DS's standard.

The DS must have sensed we were getting a bit overconfident, so they upped the enemies work rate and we got bumped twice the next night. The first was routine. A couple of shots were fired from outside the perimeter to get us standing-to for half an hour. The second time we were woken by the sound of 'whizz-bangs' (small explosive charges) being detonated in the middle of our position. The enemy had used the first probe to establish our position and were now shelling us with mortars. We hastily threw our gear in our packs and shuffled off in the darkness. I was glad I'd started to sleep with my boots on as I saw a few others in only their socks, their boots loosely stuffed into the tops of their packs.

We covered the first couple of kilometers in the dark, shuffling along the sides of the road as we attempted to put as much distance as we could between ourselves and our old position. As the darkness starting to fade, we established a quick defensive position in the undergrowth and stood-to again. The hide was tucked into the side of a densely wooded hillside, with each section laid out in a single line, side by side. As we lay in the undergrowth with the daylight spilling across the sky, the fatigue was evident on the faces around me and I struggled to keep my eyes open in the twilight. The DS walked continuously around the position and nudged anyone who looked like they might be trying to sneak in thirty-seconds of shut eye.

As the first few rays of sunshine crept through the trees, the morning light made everything glow. The fatigue had thrown my brain sideways and I felt like I was seeing things through a kaleidoscope. Amidst the paperbark trees and low-lying scrub, golden rays pierced the foliage and glimmered off the dew. I remember looking over at EJ as she sat with her back up against an old tree stump. The light swam on the surface of her rifle sight like a film of petrol on water. She looked stuffed and for once her cheeky smile had disappeared.

"What do you reckon EJ, cracking morning eh?" She squinted in the sunlight and shook her head.

"Piss off with your sunrise. I want my bed," she replied and rested her head on the butt of her rifle.

"Don't we all,' was all I could muster in response.

As luck had it, I was next up as platoon commander and dragged my pack into the center of the platoon after I'd finished morning routine. For some reason, Captain Yeoman was in good spirits and he greeted me cheerfully.

"Ahh, Cadet Rickson, welcome. Having a good morning, are we?" he grinned.

"Wouldn't be dead for quid's Sir," I replied, trying my best to sound like I was enjoying myself.

"Well, let's get on with it then. Grab your notebook and prepare to copy."

He ran through the day's mission while I furiously tried to capture the details in my grubby field notebook. After checking I had the coordinates right, he called for the section commanders and the routine started again. Even though I was dog tired, I knew there was no way of getting around it. As I waited for the section commanders to turn up, I threw back the last of the sticky-sweet coffee in my canteen and ran through the orders in my head.

"Need a hand with anything?" someone said from behind me as I crouched over my map.

I looked over my shoulder to see who it was and grinned when I saw Bensonhurst standing behind me. He had the radio slung over his shoulder and had just rotated into the platoon signaler's job. "Yeah, see if you can dial us up some bacon and egg rolls, a coffee van and the rest of the day off," I replied.

"Will do chief, but I've heard that there's a special on ration packs, leeches and rain this week. What do you reckon, want to swap?"

It was a terrible joke, but we laughed anyway. Even when you thought you had nothing left in the tank; someone would crack a joke and your spirits would lift just enough to keep you going.

"Well, call it in then mate. We'll take a double helping of the special and get them to throw in a couple of big hills too, I think we've earned it," I replied.

We were both still grinning as the section commanders appeared out of the scrub and wandered up to where we sat. With the sun well overhead, we got going again and spent the rest of the morning humping along a series of ridgelines and valleys. Captain Yeoman walked quietly beside me, occasionally checking my bearings and the positioning of the sections in the formation. From time to time, he'd offer a bit of advice or ask me what I thought about the route we'd set. Even though I felt confident, I was still pretty nervous and pulled the section commanders in each time I needed to check our position. As we patrolled, I constantly checked my map and tried to anticipate where the enemy might position themselves on each leg of the patrol. With each hill we approached, I looked for places for potential fire support positions, approach avenues and withdrawal routes. Sure enough, just before lunch we heard shots from a small clump of trees atop a small rise.

"Contact front!" the platoon yelled in unison as we hit the deck.

The forward section went through the drill, returning fire and shaking themselves out into attack formation. I could hear their section commander yelling instructions as I hustled forward towards his position.

"What have you got?" I asked.

More shots rang out from the trees, followed by a barrage of fire from the scouts.

"Two enemy, 60 meters dead ahead… two fingers left of the big pile of dead wood on the top of that hill," he replied.

I peered over the scrub, trying to get a better look. Sure enough, it was a prick of a spot to try to mount an attack as we had nothing but open country in front of us. There was limited cover along the fence line to our right and no high ground to use. I pulled my map out to see if there might be a re-entrant or gully that we could sneak into. Nothing. Captain Yeoman knelt down on the ground behind me next to Sergeant Dawson.

"What's your plan platoon commander?"

"Well, I reckon up the guts with plenty of smoke is probably out of the question," I replied.

He smiled but said nothing.

"Are you going to have a look?"

"Of course. Logan, you hold here and keep them pinned down," I replied and scurried around to the low scrub running along the fence line where I bumped into the scouts from Bravo section. KD was leaning against a large gum and chewing on a handful of crackers.

"How's it going bud?" he asked.

"Same old, same old. You see anyway we might be able to sneak around the back of these blokes," I replied and pulled my map out.

"Well, would be a long and not very much fun crawl over that paddock, but..." he offered and nodded his head down the fence.

I followed his gaze and eventually made out the hint of blue plastic in the bush along the road beside the fence. Port-a-loos.

"Seen if seen," he said with a wink.

"Seen," I replied and grinned.

I scooted back to my earlier position to find the other section commanders there with Captain Yeoman.

"Find anything?" they asked.

"Plenty," I replied and told them what I'd seen.

We poked at our maps and discussed options. The first option was a full-frontal attack across the rocky paddock, which we knew would get us there, but would suck for our mates who would have to fire and move across the open ground. The second option was to set up fire support from the fence-line and use the portaloos as a screen to move around behind the enemy. I thought it would be pressing the limits with the DS and was surprised when Captain Yeoman agreed with our plan. He had no objections to being sneaky, as his only objective was to ensure that we did our best to find, close with and kill or capture any 'enemy' we found. If they were dumb enough to position themselves so we could use the port-a-loos for cover, then they probably deserved to be dead and he urged us to get on with it. The section commanders grinned as I read out the attack plan. As they had been lucky enough to find the enemy, my old section got to sit back in fire support while the others conducted the assault. The rest of the platoon dumped their packs and quietly made their way around to the back of the port-a-loos.

Minutes later, I was poised behind Bravo section counting down the seconds until 'h-hour'. I looked up at their section commander and gave him the thumbs up. He nodded in response and passed the thumbs up to the rest of his section. Seconds later, the fire support started blasting the hill from their position, signaling the start of the assault. The rest of us silently started to move in a line towards the enemy and managed to make it almost to the base of the hill before I heard their scouts yell, "contact front!". As we assaulted towards the enemy, the air was filled with the sounds of rifle fire and the smell of cordite. Bensonhurst and I moved along behind the assaulting section, keeping pace twenty meters behind them. Off to our flank, the fire support stopped as they saw the lead section advance on the enemy's position.

"Fuck, fuck, fuck!" I heard to someone yell and looked over to see who it was. All of a sudden, I saw Possum burst out from the undergrowth, shaking his arms and kicking his legs.

Sergeant Dawson appeared behind him.

"Cadet, what the fuck are you doing?! Get back on your guts!"

The Possum either didn't hear him or didn't care. He jumped up and down, tossed his webbing and rifle on the ground and scratched furiously. Sergeant Dawson stood directly in front of him and shook his head as he realized what was going on. Somehow, he must have managed to find a firing spot right on top of an inch-ant mound. The inch-ants in this part of the world were savage critters and once they got going, you better get out of their way. I'd found that out the hard way on one of our first field exercises when I somehow managed to put my hootchie right on top of a nest of them. The little bastards could bite right through your sleeping bag and left a mark like you'd been shot with an air rifle. Dawson must have taken pity on him and started helping him swat them off, before giving him a decent serve and reminding him that he would have been dead in a real fire fight.

After another fifty meters of firing and moving our way over the rocky terrain, we were relieved to hear the DS yell "cease fire". As I shuffled forward to the center of the enemy position, I saw Hobbes helping the Possum make sure he'd got the last of the ants off as they shuffled up for the debrief. I gave him a thumbs-up and he shook his head before holding a thumb up in reply.

"Righto everyone, that's end-ex," said Captain Yeoman at the end of the debrief.

I looked around at the rest of the platoon and breathed a sigh of relief. It had been a solid week and I could see I wasn't the only one who was looking spent. After getting the nod from Captain Yeoman that my duties were done, I headed back to join my section mates. As I hitched my pack onto my back, I noticed that my shoulders no longer ached and somehow my feet felt comfortable in my dirty boots. The exercise had hardened us once again to the rigors of living in the field, replacing our soft spots with calluses and our initial clumsiness with precision as I trod quietly through the scrub.

I found the section laid on the side of the road as they started to sort through their gear in preparation for the return to barracks. Section 2IC's busied themselves reminding their sections to empty their magazines and dig out their remaining stores. Around the makeshift camp, burners happily boiled away as we made our last field brews and started stripping cam-cream off our faces.

I saw KD come bobbing along the road with Chuck, dragging hessian bags with them. After dumping them at platoon HQ, they sauntered over to us and pulled up a seat.

"Brew?" I offered.

"Does the pope shit in the woods?" said Chuck with a grin and took the offered mug.

"Not as much as Chuck does," added KD dryly.

"Piss off," replied Chuck and offered him a two-fingered salute.

"How'd you blokes go?" I asked.

"All good, I think I got through," Chuck said and handed the mug back.

"I think I'm good. More importantly, did you hear what happened at the dunnies yesterday?" KD offered.

"No, what happened?" I replied.

"You remember when we passed those port-a-loos yesterday morning? Well, Burns must have been busting, because as soon as he saw them, he did the bolt. Anyway, he gets in there, pulls the door open and jumps in with his pack on. You could hear was him banging around in there for a bit and then ..." he paused to make sure we were both listening.

"He fell out of the dunny and onto the road. Pack still on and pants half-way around his ankles! Bloody pack must have got stuck on something. The rest of us pretty much lost it on the spot."

I laughed so hard that I almost dropped my brew. Chucks shoulders danced up and down as he chuckled, both of us knew that he'd never live that down.

By the time the trucks appeared it was almost lunch, so we didn't end up back at the College till late in the afternoon. The last few hours of the exercise were spent cleaning, inspecting, re-cleaning and re-inspecting the platoon guns on the grass in front of the armoury. As we cleaned, the DS pulled us aside one by one to give us a quick debrief on our performance.

"How do you reckon you went Cadet Rickson?" Sergeant Dawson asked when it was my turn.

"Not bad sarge, I reckon I got most of it right."

He glanced at his notes and screwed his face up.

"At least I think I did," I added cautiously.

"Yeah, you did alright, but you've still got a bit to work on. You've got a pass as a section member, but then again, if you failed now you've got no hope. As section commander, you get a pass too. Next exercise remember you need to make sure your positioning puts you in the best spot to observe the upcoming terrain and communicate with the rest of the section. Don't try to be the scouts though, that's their job," he said in his usual dry manner.

"Yes, Sergeant."

"From where I stand, I reckon you managed to get through your first hook as platoon commander too. But I'll let Captain Yeoman do the rest of your debrief."

"Thanks, Sarge, appreciate it," I replied.

"Righto, off you fuck then. Next!" he said and jerked his thumb in the direction of the armoury.

Part 2. Tempus Fugit

After a quick reminder from the class duty student to make sure we all filled in the leave book and knew what time we had to be on parade in the morning, we were dismissed. As I made my way up the stairs into the company, I had my fingers crossed that the OC or Drilly had better things to do than conduct another inspection of the lines while we we'd been out field.

"What's the plan tonight?" yelled Vinny, who lived down the hall from me.

"Shower. Mess. Moose. In that order!" I yelled in reply and shot off into my room.

I was filthy, tired and ready to collapse, but it was Friday afternoon and I planned on drinking the town dry, talking rubbish and chasing a few 'civvy' girls around the dancefloor. First step was a hot shower and a set of clean clothes, followed by a quick dinner. My dirty field gear could wait until Sunday, as I wasn't going to waste a minute of Friday night doing anything that looked like hard work.

The shower block was a mass of filthy bodies and laughter as I pushed the door open.

"Jesus Poss, you look like you've been shot with a blunderbuss full of nuts and bolts," Hobbes said as Possum walked in with towel around his waist.

We all turned to look. His back and shoulders were covered with little red and purple lumps from inch-ant bites.

"Yeah, feels like it too," he replied wearily as he trudged past.

I had a few scrapes that stung when the water hit them but, on the whole, I'd escaped without too much damage. After five minutes of solid scrubbing, I'd managed to get most of the camouflage cream and assorted field dirt off me.

"Bloody hell! Put your cam cream back on, you'll break that thing," Watts said from behind me as I dried myself in front of the mirror.

"Pot this is kettle. Have you had a look at yourself lately?" I replied.

"Yep, and you know what? I'm easily the best-looking bloke in here!" he shot back with a broad grin.

With nothing more than a towel wrapped around him, Watts's normally pasty white skin was a mess of bruises and smudges of cam cream. But that didn't seem to bother him as he strutted past us and tossed his towel over the shower rail.

"You blokes might as well stay home tonight, the ladies won't want a bar of you once they see me," he called over his shoulder.

"Now that is a scary thought," Vinny replied, shaking his head.

"And you haven't even seen what he's going to wear yet," I added.

The Corps of Staff Cadets defines each of the uniform requirements that are required for every activity that cadets will undertake whilst at the College. Which is why cadets tend to stand out like sore thumbs when they are out on the town. Along with their short haircuts and rugged black watches, the uniform adoption of what is known as 'leave dress' means they are easy to pick out from the crowd in their chino's or blue jeans, polo shirts and boat shoes.

The cadets from Long Tan were no different and we looked every bit the part as we up to the mess that evening. Our checked shirts and slacks were crisply ironed, and we smelled of too much deodorant. But we felt like a million dollars and all we had on our mind was a quick bite to eat, followed by a thousand schooners.

As we trotted towards the mess, we could see the rest of the corps in their rooms unwinding from the week. The other classes had been in barracks for the week, so this was just another Friday night for them. But those of us who had returned from the field were in a celebratory mood. You could hear music blaring from various windows as our classmates readied themselves for a night on the town. Seeing as it was still early and most of us had limited funds, we were in no rush to head into the bars in town where we'd have to pay full price for our drinks. Like many of my classmates, I was perpetually broke, so my first choice of watering hole was usually the mess bar where the drinks were cheap and plentiful.

"Oi, Logan!" I yelled as we passed Alamein company.

Moments later, a head popped out of one of the rooms on the first floor.

"Who dat?" he replied.

"You coming to the mess?"

"Give me five minutes, I'll see you up there."

"Righto. Get Chuck too."

"I'll do my best, but you know him. He'll still be trying to figure out which jocks to put on!"

I gave him the thumbs up and trotted after the others who were almost at the mess steps.

"Right. Now that's done, who's thirsty?" I asked as I scraped the last bits of food off my plate.

"A man is not a camel," Walker replied and took off towards the mess bar.

"Last one there pays for the cab into town," I added and raced after him.

"Get stuffed, I still haven't had desert," Watts moaned.

"Leave it. Eating is cheating," Walker called back to him as he bounded up the stairs.

Even the threat of a couple of hours of battle PT in the morning couldn't put a dent in our mood. We knew it would be tough, but by now we thought were up for the challenge. Most of us could stagger in from town well after midnight, get a couple of hours of sleep and still be able to function in the morning. Especially when we knew that we had the rest of the day off and could make up for any lost sleep in the afternoon. After a week in the field, we thought we were ten-feet tall and bullet proof, so tomorrow could wait.

The bar was starting to get busy by the time we got there as we'd been beaten by the cadets from Alamein and Kapyong due to their proximity to the mess. Like us, they had a few solid drinkers who rarely missed a Friday night on the town. The other companies would start to appear later, as none of them seemed as excited about Friday night as we were. By the time they finished dinner, we would usually be mid-way through our fourth or fifth round. Or at least, that was our plan.

"Who wants a beer?!" I shouted as I shouldered my way to the bar. Pulling up at the front of the line, I shoved a couple of other cadets out of the way. One turned around and pushed me back.

"Fuck off Rickson, you don't own the bar," he snarled and lifted his chin.

"Bullshit, have you seen my mess bill?! I've pretty much paid for this end of the bar!" I shouted and jumped up to grab him in a headlock.

He pushed me off and straightened himself up. After the stress of the week, the pent-up testosterone and excitement had the effect of putting some people on edge. A bit of push and shove was to be expected from time to time. Sometimes it was due to a left-over grudge, but most of the time it was just because we were young and full of energy. I gave him another bit of a push and smiled.

"Save your energy for footy tomorrow mate, we're going to need it."

He grinned back and punched me in the shoulder.

"I will this time, but you owe me a beer."

"Put it on my tab," I said and laughed as I pushed through the crowd with a handful of schooners held in front of me.

"How did you blokes get on?" Logan asked as he arrived just in time to pinch one of the beers I'd set on the table.

"I got through and I'm pretty sure most of the others in our section did," I replied.

"Beauty, that's one less re-test we have to worry about!"

"I'll drink to that."

"You'll drink to anything," he replied and emptied his glass, "who wants another drink?"

"Me!" the rest of the table replied.

Two hours later and the bar was starting to get raucous. Empty glasses littered the tables and a couple of junior cadets were looking shaky on their feet. Our numbers had swollen to a dozen and we jostled for spots around the table. As the last rays of sunshine streaked across the sky above the mess, we heard whistle blasts from the duty officer that marked the 'retreat' and the end of the College day. Cadets caught outside stopped what they were doing and faced the flagpole, arms braced against their bodies. Those in the smoker's area, took a quick drag and stood fast with the lit cigarette glowing in the twilight beside them.

The best way to get into town on a Friday night was to score a lift from one of the cadets that was catching up on work or didn't drink. Both of which were pretty rare, but luckily for us, Walker had already tapped one of the blokes from our company on the shoulder for this purpose. After finishing what drinks were left on the table, someone made the call that next drinks would be downstairs Moose in twenty minutes. At this time of night, not even the most conscientious OC or Drilly would be wandering the lines so we hooted and hollered as we jogged back to the lines. Walker ran ahead and tapped on one of the windows on the ground floor, alerting our driver to the fact that his wheels were needed. Minutes later we crammed into his car and made the turn out of the company carpark at speed.

On the way to town, we played corners, smashing each other into the side of the car as we sped around each of the big roundabouts that dotted the Canberra landscape. Pulling off the big roundabout before we entered Civic, someone shouted, "Chinese fire drill!" and we all roared with laughter. We could see the next set of lights start to go orange as we sped passed the convention center. The sounds of seatbelts being unbuckled could be heard as Morris started to apply the brakes. In the front Walker held up a hand with the fingers cross, the field signal for '30 seconds to go' and we braced against each door.

"Are you guys serious?!" Morris moaned as the car came to a halt and we all jumped out.

A 'Chinese fire drill' was simple. When pulling up at a set of lights, all of the occupants of the car had to get out and run a lap of the car before the lights changed. When done with another cadet driving it was a bit of fun, but when done in a taxi, it was even more hilarious as the cabbie thought you were doing a runner before he realized that you were all getting back in the car. Bonus points were awarded for the nude version of the drill, although this was rarely achieved when taking a cab. Cordy traditions like this were passed down over the years with the expectation that we would keep them alive. Like many of the cordy traditions, no-one knew who started it, but no-one questioned its validity. All we knew was that it was a tradition and that it was our job to keep it alive, so we did.

We all laughed madly and slapped each other on the back as we jumped back into the car for the last stretch of the drive.

"Are you coming in? Come on, don't be a soft. I'll even buy you a drink," I yelled from the backseat as we pulled up.

Our driver smiled politely and told us that he had some study to do, so we let him off with a quick thanks and a bang on the roof as we ran across London Circuit towards the neon lights of Mooseheads Tavern.

Dan Henricson

Mooseheads Tavern aka The Moose

Like every good training institution, the College had a few local watering holes where cadets could go to blow off some steam from their weeks duties. Of these, the most popular over the years was Mooseheads Tavern. The Moose, as it became known, first opened its doors in Canberra in the late 80's and fast became the drinking place of choice for cadets from the College and Defence Academy. During the day, it was a watering hole for local government workers and an assortment of Canberra blow-ins, but they dwindled away as night fell and the hordes of cadets descended on the place.

The Moose was a safe haven from the instructors, College rules and the hierarchy. Rank no longer mattered at the Moose and a punch-on there was considered fair play. If you were playing up and got knocked on your arse, the fight was over. The winner claimed their spot at the bar and the loser headed off to one of the other bars down the street. Whether we had something to celebrate or something to commiserate, we went to The Moose.

...

We bounded across the road and through the front doors of The Moose with grins on our faces. I hit the bar first and ordered a round of drinks while the boys looked for real estate. Getting in early not only meant we could get a seat, but we could also skip the line to get upstairs later on in the night. The bouncers were a tough bunch who put up with us most of the time but had no objection with tossing us out if we got unruly. This rarely happened as most cadets showed the place the same respect that they did the mess bar. Plus, they knew that if you screwed up too many times you'd get barred for the rest of the year.

As the night wore on, the place heaved with bodies until it was shoulder to shoulder. At some stage someone suggested we head upstairs and after that the rest of the night became a bit of a blur.

The upstairs dance floor was a sweaty, psychedelic experience filled with loud music and strobe lights. As we drank, danced and sweated the night away, we ignored our watches in an attempt to forget about the coming day. By now our training had instilled in us a sense of belief that we could handle anything. When combined with youth and alcohol, it created a cocoon of invincibility that let us think tomorrow would never come.

At some point long past midnight the music stopped abruptly, and the fluorescent lights were turned on.

"Fuck me, I think I've gone blind," I said, blinking my eyes.

Looking around me, I could make out a handful of cordy's amongst the thinning crowd. The floor was sticky from spilled drinks and empty glasses littered the tables and bar tops.

"I think that's the signal for end of exercise," Watts mumbled.

"Yep, we're cooked. Let's get out of here," I agreed.

He threw an arm over my shoulder and we staggered down the stairs. The night air cold chipped away at our drunkenness as marched doggedly around towards the taxi rank.

"Have we got time for a hot-dog before we go home?"

The big fella always needed food and by asking he knew there was a chance he'd get us to detour on the way.

"I'm not fussed," I replied, trying my best to put one foot in front of the other.

We turned towards The Bin nightclub's hotdog stand, which was considered a mandatory stop for anyone who was still out when the ugly lights came on. Minutes later, with bin-dogs in hand, we happily stumbled back to the cab stand and did our best to ignore the morning parade that was now only hours away.

The first thing I heard in the morning was the sound of doors opening and closing. Immediately I knew I had slept in.

"Fuck!" I mumbled and scrambled out of bed.

Surveying my room, it took a second to figure out what time it was and what was going on. I poked my head out of the door and saw the rest of the company exiting their rooms in their battle PT gear.

"Fuck!" I mumbled again.

Looking down on the floor of my room, I saw my cam pants, company jersey and boots laid out for me. Damn, I was smart when I was pissed, I thought. Looking over to my desk, I saw my keys, pain killers and water bottle. Good work, I reminded myself. It took me less than two minutes to throw my gear on, grab a couple of pain killers and a swig of water. If nothing else, the College taught us the value of being prepared. I tossed my keys into my pocket, chucked my webbing on, grabbed my rifle out of its lock and raced out the door.

"Hey, any of you blokes know what time we got home last night?" Vinny asked as we ran down the stairs.

"Nighttime!" I yelled as I ran after him.

In front of me, Watts, Walker and Hobbes all laughed.

"Fuck, I think I'm still pissed," added Watts.

"Given what we had to drink last night, we'll be pissed until Wednesday," Hobbes chimed in.

Each company had its own form of Saturday morning torture, as it was the only time the OC had the entire company to themselves. No Drilly. No CO. Just us and them, for a bit of 'one on one' time. With his love of all things soldiering, our OC had decided that the best thing we could be doing on a Saturday morning was honing our skills in the art of 'bayonet fighting'. Looking up the hill, I could see the cadets from Gallipoli heading towards the obstacle course and the poor bastards from Alamein forming up on the drill square. The other companies must have pulled a lucky straw and ended up with something indoors. What I wouldn't give to swap with them, I thought.

After forming up out front of the company and calling the roll, the CSM gave us a reminder to put in our best efforts before handing over to the OC. In his customary manner, the OC didn't stuff around and had us double-timing down the road straight away.

"Left, right, left, right, left," he yelled as we ran past the CO's house.

"Left, right, left, right, left," we echoed, our steps matching the cadence.

My head pounded as the soles of my boots bounced off the pavement. As we ran, I hoped the rest of the party animals were suffering the same fate I was. Looking across at my classmates, I could see Watts already looking grey. Next to him, Vinny was sweating bullets and I could see Hobbes face turning red as he huffed and puffed between strides.

"Hi ho, it's off work we go," sang Walker as we turned off towards the football ovals.

"Fuck off with your hi-ho, hi-ho," Watts slurred, his face looking pastier by the minute.

"This will do you a world of good buddy. Sweat out the rum from last night and make room for a few more tonight!" he replied with a grin.

Walker always managed to pull up alright after a big night and he smiled as he bounced along to the cadence. I did my best to keep a grin on my face, but my legs felt heavy and all I could think about was crawling back into bed after we finished.

"I'm not drinking with you blokes ever again," Watts wheezed.

"And again, and again and again..." Hobbes and I chorused.

Wearing webbing and carrying a rifle, we were expected to cover a kilometer in roughly seven minutes. In full field kit, the same distance would take us roughly double the time, whilst in standard PT gear it was expected to take less than five. Today, it took us exactly seven minutes as Captain Sala kept us in precise double-time all the way to the ovals. The oval still had a light dew on it as we changed from double-time to quick-time and then halted alongside the pines that separated the golf course from the footy ovals. The run had somewhat cleared up my vision, even though my head still pounded, and my stomach still hadn't decided whether it was going to play the game for the morning's activities. The sweat that had built up on my brow seemed far away, as the remnants of last night's alcohol still coursed its way through my veins. Looking around, the rest of the company seemed bright eyed and bushy tailed in comparison. I'm never drinking again, I thought to myself as I listened to the OC tell us about the history of bayonet fighting. He reminded us of the great feats achieved by Australian soldiers on the rugged battlefields of the first and second World Wars. We were already familiar with stories of many of these battles after our trip to the War Memorial and we understood the importance of being able to master the same skills that our soldiers were expected to perform, including bayonet fighting.

The challenge many of us had was understanding the relevance to the modern battlefield we were all being prepared for. A battlefield controlled by artillery barrages, close air-support, tanks and machine guns, didn't seem to have much need for bayonets. Especially ones as blunt as our issued 'pig stickers'. Like many soldiers who had gone before us, we had trouble comprehending the complexity of war, let alone what it would be like to kill some in hand-to-hand fighting. Whilst we yearned for the adventure that an overseas deployment offered and trusted in our training to prepare us for the 'two-way range', none of us had any real idea how we'd react on a battlefield.

If nothing else, our military history lessons had taught us that mankind had always managed to resort to brutality when it came to the pointy end of the battlefield. It rarely mattered which side you were on or what the motives were, rules didn't count when you were faced with an enemy in close proximity. Looking around my classmates, I knew there were more than a few who looked forward to the opportunity to test themselves on a real battlefield. However, I was also pretty sure that the rigorous psychological testing that we had undertaken in order to get here ensured that most of us were not, in fact, psychopaths who looked forward to stabbing another person with a blunt knife on the end of a rifle.

"In – out – on guard!!" the OC yelled at the front of the company as he demonstrated how we were expected to disembowel our enemy with a straight thrust to the stomach. Bayonet drills were always accompanied by a series of commands that we yelled at the top of our voice. Scenes from *Full Metal Jacket* ran through my head as we yelled and ran at our targets with our best 'war faces' on. We stabbed and slashed our way through the next hour, alternating the bayonet drills with laps of the oval and physical training exercises designed to toughen our bodies and minds in preparation for war. At the end of the training the OC looked on us approvingly and handed us back to the CSM to double-time back to the lines.

"Jesus, I think I can smell the rum in your sweat," I said to Watts as we jogged back.

"Lucky that session didn't go for another minute," he replied between paces, "Or you would have been able to see it too!"

The big guy had a delicate stomach and was known for his mid-PT chunders at the gym or various training fields. Those around him sniggered and smiled, glad that someone else was deeper in the hurt locker than they were.

After being fallen out in front of the lines, the company dispersed back into the building in dribs and drabs. Most headed straight back to their rooms to stow their rifles and hit the showers, while a few others opted for a soft drink and a cigarette outside the laundry. The rest of the day was allocated to sport, so I was planning on a long hot shower and another hour in the farter before I did anything.

"Rickson, what time did you get back in last night?" the Platoon Sergeant asked as I walked back to my room.

"Dunno, why?" I replied.

"Well, I'm hoping you didn't forget to sign back in when you got back... I heard the OC was on his way to check the leave book," she replied curtly.

Although she came off pretty tough, our Platoon Sergeant, cadet Duncan, was fair, and her warning was well intentioned. She knew I was already on the OC's shit list and any further black marks would eventually end up in a charge.

"Fuck!" I replied and shook my head.

I searched through my scrambled memories from last night to try to remember whether I'd checked back in when we got back to the lines. I remember stumbling out of the cab and fumbling for the keys to my room, but everything else was hazy after that. The hairs started to crawl on the back of my neck, and I felt that sticky pre-sweat feeling on my back as I realized that I probably hadn't signed in and had forgotten to do it this morning after sleeping through my alarm. I bolted downstairs to the foyer where the leave book was kept. The company orderly, cadet Bates was there and had the leave book under her arm.

"Hey mate, can I just check the leave book before you go?" I asked as I skidded up to her.

"Sorry, can't do. The OC wants it, now," she replied.

"Don't be a jack, it will only take a minute," I said, pissed that she had not offered it up immediately.

After all, it was expected that you look after your mates and being jack was an easy way to earn the scorn of all of both classmates and DS alike.

"What's going on out there Bates? Bring that leave book in here," boomed the OC's voice from inside his office.

Bates looked at me sheepishly, shrugged her shoulders and replied, "Nothing sir, coming."

Knowing that she didn't have a choice meant I had no reason to be pissed off, but it didn't help as I knew I was in deep shit. Again.

I watched Bates march into the OC's office and walked back to my room. Whilst my body was tired and needed rest, my mind was running in circles thinking about the inevitable ass-kicking that was surely on its way. I bumped into Walker on the way back to my room.

"Hey mate, did you remember to sign in last night when we got back?" I asked.

"Nah, but I went down and fixed it first thing this morning," he replied.

"Did you sign me back in?"

"Shit, no mate. I was in such a hurry that I didn't think to check. Are you sure you didn't do it when you got back?"

"I don't know for sure, but I think I'm in the shit as the OC's got the book now," I said with a sigh.

"Don't stress mate, not signing the leave book isn't a major offence. You'll probably just end up with a few more showies and a couple of extra days on the shit list" he said optimistically.

"I wish mate. The OC's been looking for an opportunity to bust me for a while now and I'm guessing this will do it. Ahh well, what's the worst thing they can do, take my birthday off me?" I said with a half-hearted grin.

The military discipline system was part of our curriculum and it was expected that a few cadets in each class would be charged with one of the multitude of offences that could be committed at the College. Most of them were variations on the same theme, 'disobeying a lawful general order', which was essentially not following the rules set out in barracks orders. During our classes on military law, we had come to learn that there was a section for just about every misdemeanor you could think of. As junior officers we were expected to know the ins and outs of the military discipline system so we could enforce them, and like many of the things we were taught, we learned as much by doing as we did by reading about it. Using this reckoning, most of my classmates figured that I would be an expert in military law by the time I graduated.

After OC's parade, Saturdays at the College were devoted to participating in sport of some kind. All cadets were expected to play at least one sport and take part in the intra-company competitions. It was meant to build character and help us become better team players but was also a great way to blow off a bit of steam from the long weeks of training. It also didn't hurt that most sporting events ended up at the bar.

Of the sports played at the College, rugby was still considered by many to be the only game that counted. Contact sports have always been a part of military life, for they provide a place for young men and women to forge their characters and develop relationships with their peers. This was no different at the College and rugby was seen as a great building block for individual toughness and a dedication to the team. The College teams club might not have been the biggest on the paddock, but they were fit, tough and disciplined. Many of the cadets had come from the traditional rugby schools, so there was always plenty of competition for spots across the field. The rugby teams also sported members of the instructors as rank did not carry onto the field, the only things that counted were individual skill and commitment to the team. This provided a good opportunity for the instructors to get to know the cadets better and for those cadets that played well to earn the respect of the staff. The 'rugby assist' was also a good way to boost your chances of getting through your assessments, hence any cadet who knew how to play the game would be seen at rugby try-outs at the start of each season. Having come straight from boarding school, I had come to love the game with a semi-religious fervor as rugby summed up my attitude to life. Play hard, look after your mates and when the game was over, play even harder. Unfortunately, I was out for the season as I'd injured myself early in the year, which made it tough having to sit on the sidelines each week.

Today the club was playing at home, so we didn't need to do anything until just before 3rd grade kicked off at 1300. By the time the whistle blew for 1st grade the hill would be packed with cadets, staff and any old boys who were posted locally. For home games, the club ran a beer and BBQ tent, which was staffed by cadets. If you had friends in the beer tent, five dollars went a long way.

My plan was to get a couple of hours of extra farter in after PT and head down for the end of the 2nd grade game, but after my run in with the OC I couldn't get to sleep. I figured the best medicine for a hang-over was another one, so I threw on my College blazer and grabbed the loose change from my top drawer before heading off to the footy fields. On the walk to the oval, I saw a familiar shape sauntering along ahead of me.

"Oi, wait up," I called.

KD turned around to see who it was. The AFL club had a bye this week, so must have been heading down to watch the rugby as an excuse to partake in a few cheap beers. Like me, he was also perennially broke, and he knew how that the best way to stretch his remaining dollars was to see if the cadets on bar duty might help him out.

"What did you blokes do for OC's parade this morning?" I asked as I drew alongside him.

He stepped off alongside me, making sure his strides were in-time with mine just in case one of the instructors or senior cadets might be driving past.

"Mil history presentation on the battle of Cannae," was his reply.

"Where the hell is that?" I said in response.

"Egypt, I think. Something to do with the Romans. I was too hungover to pay much attention. Good bludge though as there was no test and all of the questions were answered by one of fourthies who is into that sort of thing," he said with a smile.

"Luck buggers, we had bloody bayonet training. You could have got drunk on the rum fumes coming off us. I was rooted by the time we were done."

"Yeah, your OC takes his job way too seriously. Ex-diggers cannot be trusted," he said and shook his head.

"Well talk about taking it too seriously, I'm pretty sure he's going to bust me for not signing the leave book when I got in last night. I tried to sign in when we got back from training, but he was already back in the company," I said in between steps.

"Sounds like you're screwed then. Sounds like three days ROPs and seven days confined to barracks?"

"Yeah, that's what I figure. Hey, what's the chances you could be my defending officer? My Platoon Sergeant has offered, but I reckon I could do with a mate in the court room."

KD thought about it for a minute and shook his head. He had a solid grasp on most of subjects and seemed to breeze through the lessons and assessments. At the same time, he liked to question the logic behind much of the theory, as he often found it to be old fashioned and behind the times. Yet, somehow, he managed to escape the ire of the Drilly's and rest of the DS, and his company mates had nicknamed him 'Teflon' in reference to the fact that shit never seemed to stick.

"You're in the shit for sure and there isn't a defense officer alive who will get you off that. Your OC has a hard-on for busting people and by the sounds of it, you're on the top of his list. But we might just be able to throw a bit of sand in his eye whilst we're at it," he said with another of his trademark grins.

I nodded in agreement, and knew he was right. Even for a pretty minor offence, I was going to get the book thrown at me. I knew I should do what all cadets were expected to do in these situations and lie down and take my punishment quietly. Learn the lesson, make sure I didn't repeat the mistake again and use the opportunity to better understand the Defence Force Discipline Act (DFDA). But like my friend, I also had a logic cog somewhere that didn't quite mesh with the DFDA and led to question the system far too often. It wasn't that I didn't think the military needed discipline. I fully understood its criticality in maintaining the chain of command and codes of conduct. But the application of the disciplinary systems purely for punishment reminded me of the saying my dad had taught me, "If the only tool you have is a hammer, then every problem you have is a nail". In my case, this almost guaranteed that at some stage I was going to end up as one of those nails.

We discussed my chances of getting charged as we rounded the golf course and headed down to the main rugby oval. By the time we got there KD had agreed that he'd defend me and had already started formulating a plan for the trial. At that moment it seemed like a very good idea and we thought we might even 'Perry Mason' our way out of the charge. Even though I knew I was more than likely going to get the book thrown at me, having KD beside me when it happened would make the process a hell of a lot less painful. Feeling a lot happier about the situation, I felt my hangover start to lift and my thoughts turned to rugby and a cold beer.

As a member of the club, you were expected to turn up early and help out setting up the ground. Setting up was more favorable to packing up at the end of the game, as by then we'd be in a hurry to get back to the mess bar. According to the unwritten rules of College life, if you helped with set-up you were well within your rights to say you'd done your bit for the day. Besides setting up the posts, pads and putting out the bins, there was always the matter of putting up the beer and BBQ tents. Whilst this seemed to be a very simple exercise, the art of assembling an Army issued 11-by-11 tent was often anything but and had been known to cause the occasional fisty-cuffs when you got had a couple of young males in the group who wouldn't accept someone else telling them what to do.

The process started by dragging the folded sections of the tents out of storage and laying them alongside the structure, which consisted of a number of deceptively sized steel poles and joints. From there you were supposed to build the roof first, over which you draped the tent body and then lifted it up one side at a time to add the legs. Due to the seeming simplicity of the task, cadets would rush into the job and start throwing together the sections independently before realizing they had stuffed up at one end or the other. The resulting re-assembly included a number of poles being put in the wrong spot, which required another round of re-assembly. By this stage a few of the original workers would have decided it was too much effort and skulked off to find an easier job. If there were any of the instructors around, one of them would eventually take charge and start barking orders.

"That's the side fuck-knuckle, grab the end!"

"Turn the bloody tarp around you numpties and pull it over from the other side!"

After the application of a number of helpful phrases, the tents would eventually end up assembled, tied down and turned around to face the oval. Once set up, the tents we filled with esky's and tables so we could serve the hordes of thirsty cadets who would descend over the next few hours. I volunteered for a turn at the bar for the first half of 3rd grade as it was usually pretty quiet early on.

"Ahh, Cadet Rickson I see you're pulling your weight behind the bar instead of in front of it for a change," said Sergeant Ruth with a smile as he sauntered up to the bar.

"Yes Sergeant, I thought I'd see how the other half live," I quipped in response.

Sergeant Ruth usually played in 2nd grade but was out this game as we'd been in the field for the week and was giving one of the 3rd

College Blues

class blokes a run in his spot. He pulled up at the far end of the bar and motioned me over.

"Now, I hear you're in the shit again. What's the story?" he said quietly.

"Good news travels fast I guess," I replied casually.

He looked about to see who was around and seeing no one, looked back at me with a steely gaze.

"Righto, keep your trap shut for the next minute and listen up. I keep hearing your name around the Sergeant's mess and not for anything good. Your Drilly now has you first, second and third on his shit list, which is not good for you or your graduation chances... Now, from what I'm told, you're not a fucking idiot, so you should be breezing through training. But instead, you keep putting your neck out and rubbing people up the wrong way," he said putting his weight onto the bar table and making the timbers groan.

"Now if you were one of my diggers, I'd have you running hills until you sorted your shit out. But you aren't, so I can't. So, instead I'm just going to say this. If you want to graduate with your mates, then I'd suggest you cut the shit from here on in and get on with it. I want you to become a fucking grey man. So grey that I almost forget you exist. Got it?" he said and stood up to his full height.

By now I had braced myself up and simply nodded in reply. I knew this was meant to be an arse-kicking, but it was also showed that there were a few DS that did want us to get through.

"Righto, now grab me a couple of heavies and let's crack on with some footy," he said with a wry smile.

After he left, I saw the other cadets looking at me.

"What was that about?" one of them asked.

"I'm in the shit again. I'm pretty sure the OC is going to charge me for not signing the leave book," I replied and shrugged my shoulders.

"What do you mean? Hardly anyone in our company signs the bloody leave book!" he said and threw up his hands.

"Exactly. You reckon that'll hold up in court?" I said and we both laughed.

By the time the siren sounded for 1st grade to run on, the sun was low on the horizon and winter's icy breath could be felt as it settled around us. I was sitting on the hill with KD, Logan and the boys from 3rd grade, and we clapped and hooted as the team ran out. The team always looked a little lopsided with the fresh-faced cadets looking out of place next to the larger shapes of the instructors. We cheered each time our team scored or managed to go close as the two teams belted their way up and down the field. Noses were bloodied and bodies bruised, as the country boys did their best to remind the cadets that they still had plenty to learn about the game, particularly what happens when you get caught on the bottom of the ruck. The occasional flare-ups that looked like they might spark into a brawl were quickly pulled-up by one of the instructors who reminded the cadets that they represented the Army whilst on the field and that the Commandant was also amongst the spectators. The strength of College sporting teams lay in their fitness, willingness to stick up for each other and the fact that they were more disciplined than their opponents. This last component was often preyed upon by opposing teams who knew cadets were banned from fighting, lest they be disciplined off the field. So, you got used to the occasional swinging arm or stray boot when you were on the ground and remembered the mantra that was drilled into us by the coaches, "look at the scoreboard". Just as we were expected to do on the battlefield, our focus was on the team and the end result was always considered more important than getting our pride dented.

The last rays of sunshine stained the clouds pink and orange as the final whistle blew. The scoreboard told us we had been victorious, and the College team formed a tunnel for the other team as a show of good sportsmanship. Even though the game had been fierce in patches and many of our players were sporting the results, all was forgotten now the final whistle had sounded. Whilst this wasn't always reciprocated by our opposition, it was an important part of College tradition. It reminded us that we were training to be officers, and as leaders we were expected to lead by example, both on and off the field. This wasn't always easy, as there was often plenty of niggle from opposing teams who knew we were unlikely to retaliate. But the expectation remained that we would remain in control of ourselves, as losing control meant you lost sight of the bigger picture.

Our merry band from the hill stumbled back to the mess as soon as the siren sounded. We managed to sneak away with a haul of cheap beers crammed into the various pockets of our blazers, which clinked away as we attempted to keep ourselves in step on the march back to the lines. By the time we reached the mess we were well and truly pissed, but like the hardened drinkers that we were, we were a long way from being done for the night.

With the last sporting teams returning to barracks, the mess bar was a boiling pot of red faces, loud voices and loose hormones. Each sport tended to stick within their groups, as each group had its own culture and characters. The non-contact sports tended to be quieter and sat in small circles discussing sport and other more serious topics. The footy teams, rugby and AFL, in contrast were louder and looser. Even though it was frowned upon, there was always a fair bit of mixing between the male and female cadets after game days. There were no obvious displays of affection in the mess though, as this was still considered out-of-bounds. But as the night progressed, anyone with a keen eye would have spotted the occasional cadets sneak away for a stealthy rendezvous in the lines. On occasion someone would be dispatched to the lines to check on them, as many still considered 'fratting' to be unacceptable, particularly if it meant leaving your mates in the bar when it was their shout.

"Righto, who's coming to town?" Olly demanded from the other side of the table.

"Love to mate, but I'm broke till next payday," I said.

Looking around, I could see a few heads nodding along as most of us were down to our last few dollars by the second weekend after payday. With the exception of ex-soldiers, cadets weren't paid much and most of us considered it our duty to spend most of our pay on taxi fares, booze and bin-dogs. Hence, the second weekend after pay week usually meant the chances of ending up at the mess and then in someone's room for a sneaky after-hours drink was better than average.

"Well, I'm not sitting around here all night," said KD, "Let's grab some drinks and head back to my room."

"Good plan, I'll get the drinks," I replied.

"Fuck Kokoda, that's too far to walk," chimed in Logan, "Why don't you blokes come down my way and we'll see if we can't sneak into the room."

By this stage of the proceedings anything that involved more drinks sounded like a good idea. Anything that also involved breaking the rules while simultaneously keeping one of the College traditions alive was an even better idea. We polished off a few more beers and convinced the barman to let us put a couple of bottles of cheap port on our mess bills, which we hid under our jackets as we stumbled down the mess steps and into the cold night air.

The Room in a Room

Of all the traditions of the College, few are more revered than holding a porto's (drinking session) in the 'room in a room'. The room itself is, as the name suggests, inside one of the other rooms, or underneath it to be more accurate. The hollow space under the floorboards was excavated by industrious cadets in the late 1950's as a place to stash their dirty gear during inspections. The room remains set up as a normal room, although no cadets have been assigned to live in it since it's discovery. It no longer serves as a stash spot for dirty gear and is kept as a testament to the ingenuity of the cadets who built it.

...

Climbing down the five short steps that lead down into the room, I heard Logan say, "watch your head," just in time to avoid banging my head against the wooden beam that protruded from the floorboards. Over the years the old wooden floor supports had caught many a cadet off-guard as they climbed down into the shallow room. Ducking under the supports I handed Logan the bottle of port I had in my jacket and yelled, "Clear!" to let KD know I was off the ladder.

The room was just over a meter deep, so we were forced to crawl on our hands and knees once we were in it. The dim light of an old exposed light bulb gave the place the ambiance of one of those tunnels you'd see in a war movie. As I settled onto the filthy carpet, I saw KD's feet hit the bottom of the ladder and heard the 'clunk' of his head as it found the bearer.

"Fuck!" he cursed, and I heard Logan laugh behind me.

"Sorry mate," I said, realizing I should have warned him.

"Jesus, she's tight down here," quipped KD as he shuffled in and plonked down beside me.

Logan opened the port and splashed it into one of the mugs that he'd grabbed from the company kitchen on the way. The sticky aroma of cheap port filled in the air as we clinked our mugs together. Like most cadets, port was something we had been introduced to via the traditions of the Army dining-in, where it accompanied the toasts that were offered at the end of the night. Whilst good port can be magic stuff, showing off both the art of the wine maker and the quality of the grapes, the stuff we drank was far from that. The port from the mess was cheap and nasty, but it didn't seem to bother us one bit.

Midway through the second bottle, we heard someone stomping down the hallway, so we stopped talking and listened, in case it was one of the senior cadets who might decide to poke their head in on the festivities. Even though the room in a room was considered communal property and any parties in it were generally ignored, there was the occasional 1st class cadet who took things a bit too seriously. Getting caught usually resulted in being told to pack up and F-off back to your own lines. Worst case you might end up with an extra duty or two, but generally unless you were being too loud or making a mess, you were left alone. The footsteps in the hall grew louder and were punctuated by the occasional thump or two as the culprit bumped down the hall.

"Sounds like someone is blind," whispered Logan.

The footsteps continued thumping along the hall until they were right above us. We could hear some scratching about above us before a heavily accented voice called down to us from the stairs, "Hey, you blokes got anything to drink?"

We knew the voice and knew it couldn't mean anything but trouble, as it was almost certainly one of the Fijians who we knew loved a drink.

"Depends, how much money have you got?" KD yelled back.

"What?! None. I'm broke like you blokes," came the response, which was immediately followed by a set of feet descending the ladder.

His feet had barely connected with the floor when we heard the solid thump of his head connecting with the overhead beam. Thump! We looked at each other and laughed.

"Bloody hell, that thing gets me every time!" he stammered as he rubbed his head.

"Pass that man a bottle," Logan said and handed him the half empty bottle.

He tossed back a solid swig and slumped onto the floor next to me. Dave was a happy go-lucky fellow who wasn't much chop at the academic side of things, but he was solid in the field and handy on the footy paddock. As classmates, they were good to have around in the field as they didn't complain about humping a few extra stores or carrying the gun. In barracks, they were amongst the first at the bar and could always be relied on to play a few tunes when guitar could be found. They loved a drink and you had to watch yourself if you got caught in a shout with them, as drinking was a semi-professional sport for them.

"Where did you come from mate?" Logan asked.

"Ahhh, you know... we had a few drinks at the oval then we took a case back to my room," he replied and pulled on the bottle again.

"Well, just remember, if you go to sleep in here, I'm not bloody carrying you out," Logan said and grinned.

"Ahhh, fuck it, if I sleep here you leave me here," was his reply and we weren't going to disagree with him.

Which was lucky as by the time the second bottle was empty, he was snoring loudly and none of us was up carrying him back up the stairs. We left the light on and stumbled off back to our own rooms, glad we weren't waiting in a freezing cab line and looking forward to the warmth of our beds.

I woke up Sunday morning to the sounds of birds. The hustle and bustle of the rest of the week was replaced by an almost eerie silence as the College rested. The only parade on Sunday was the weekly church service but this had long ago ceased to be a compulsory activity. Given the chance between attending church or sleeping in, it was a better chance that unless you were a member of the truly devoted, you'd take the latter option. The church still retained an important place in the Army as a number of units still had their own chaplain. Throughout history, soldiers have often held a reverence for one God or another, possibly due to the fact that death seems so much closer on the battlefield. We were often reminded that there are no atheists in foxholes, but like many young people who had not seen the battlefield or been faced with our own mortality, we paid these comments lip service as we figured that when the time came, we would make up our own mind.

Either way, my Sunday was free as I had no punishments or parades to attend besides the usual afternoon of cleaning in preparation for Monday morning's BC Day parade. As I was too late for breakfast in the mess, the next best thing was to see if I could scrape together enough loose change out of my top drawer for a run into town for some fast food. After scratching through my drawers and the jeans I'd worn on Friday night, I managed to gather what looked like enough, so I grabbed my car keys and headed out to the carpark. On the way out I saw Watts walking back from the mess casually. When he saw me heading towards my car, he sped up to catch me.

"You going to town?" he said with a grin.

"Yeah, missed breakfast so I'm doing a run into town," I replied.

"Sweet, can I get a lift?"

I could see the remnants of what looked like tomato sauce on his shirt and knew he rarely missed breakfast.

"Haven't you already had a feed?" I asked as I unlocked the door of my old ute.

"Of course, but I've always got room for seconds," he said and ran around to the passenger side.

"Jesus mate, I don't know where you put it," I replied with a grin, even though I knew exactly where he put it.

The engine wound over a few times before it caught and spluttered to life. Black smoke puffed out of the tailpipe as the old diesel didn't like the cooler weather much. Watts wound the window down and hung his arm out as I gunned it past the parade ground and towards the main gates.

"How was last night? You weren't one of the blokes drinking in the room in a room last night, were you?" he asked as we turned out of the main gates.

"Yeah, maybe... Did someone dob us in?" I said and felt the hairs on the back of my neck prickle.

"Nah, you blokes are alright, but I heard one of the Fijians fell asleep in there and the CSM found him this morning after he heard him snoring. Found the bottles of port beside him and gave him a couple of extra's for it," Watts said with a smile.

"He didn't say anything about the rest of us then?"

"Not from what I heard, sounds like you might have dodged a bullet. For once."

I quietly thanked myself for pulling the plug when I did and heading back to my room. Even though I felt sorry for Dave for getting caught, I was glad it was someone else for a change.

Along with the rest of my classmates, I spent the rest of the day trying to find things to take my mind off the Monday morning inspection and putting off any preparation until the last possible minute. By mid-afternoon, it became clear that my room wasn't going to clean itself and I resigned myself to the fact that I'd have to get started. The Monday morning inspection required everything in our room to be dust free, spotless and polished to the hilt. Any non-issued equipment had to be stripped off our field gear, rifles were broken down and thoroughly cleaned, boots spit-polished until we could see our faces in them, and uniforms ironed in regulation manner. If you were lucky, the inspection would be conducted by your Platoon Sergeant. If you were less lucky, you got the CSM, and if you were shit-out-of-luck, you got the Drilly or the OC. I knew I was far from lucky, so I figured my chances of at least getting the CSM were better than average and I was an even chance of getting the Drilly or OC. Like most cadet who had gone before me, I hated the Sunday bogging sessions more than anything. But I hated re-inspections and extra duties more, so I grabbed a brew and got on with it.

There's a theory in the Army that there is nothing that cannot be ironed, polished or dusted. This included the soles of your running shoes, the hinges on the inside of your cupboard and just about any horizontal surface. If a human finger could reach inside, underneath, around or on top of any object, it was able to be subjected to inspection. We were expected to have every single item in our room up to inspection standard and knew that a thorough inspecting officer would work hard to find a fine layer of dust, the hint of carbon, bootlaces that weren't aligned or socks that weren't 'smiling' in your drawer. The most common items for inspection were always the big ones; boots, brass, rifle, uniforms and horizontal surfaces, hence they drew the most focus. Invariably, at some stage during the bogging process you'd be interrupted by one of your mates who was going stir crazy as they continuously polished their parade boots or thrust their fingers into the breach of their rifle, chasing the finest elements of grit around. On the promise that we'd take a quick five minutes break, you'd pull up stumps and stop to bitch about what a pain in the backside inspections were. Inevitably, this would turn into twenty then thirty minutes as you procrastinated for as long as possible. Which only resulted in not finishing until almost midnight and telling yourself, "Next week, I'm definitely starting earlier...".

I knew that, as I told myself this every week and yet still ended up at some stage on a Sunday night making a decision as to which outstanding items in the room would be left to chance. Tonight, was

College Blues

no different and the glowing red numbers on my alarm clock said it was just after midnight by the time I was in bed.

It didn't matter what time I set my alarm on Monday mornings, I always woke up well before it, afraid I would sleep in and lose precious minutes of preparation time. After roll call and a quick breakfast (if you had time), the routine was the same. First was the three S's and a quick brew on the run. Pull out your parade uniform and leave it hanging up, so it didn't get creased while you did a final check of your room. Next, you wiped down all the horizontal surfaces again and checked to make sure you had hidden anything that wasn't up to inspection standard. Brass was laid out on your table from the night before and you gave that a quick look over before pulling your rifle out. Once it was stripped and laid out on your bed, you pulled the barrel through once more just in case it had collected any dust overnight. Finally, you ran through each cupboard and drawer, making sure your uniforms were all facing the same direction and that they were all in order. Inevitably during this last check, you would realize that you'd missed something. If it wasn't critical, you would look for somewhere to hide it. If it was, you either gave it a quick once over or just prayed whoever was doing the inspection wouldn't find it. If you knew it was bad enough though, you had no choice but to spend the remaining time worrying about it. At the last possible minute, you got dressed and stowed any cleaning gear before standing outside your room.

Looking down the hall, I could see the rest of the cadets in our platoon outside their doors, standing at ease and waiting for the Platoon Sergeant to bring us to attention. Across the hall from me I could see the Possum shuffle from foot to foot in his nervous manner.

"You right Poss?" I whispered.

"All good," he sniffed in reply, "but I've lost one of my water bottles somewhere, so I'm one short on my pack."

"Fuck mate, why didn't you say something earlier," I shot back and checked my watch.

We were inside the one-minute mark, but I knew I had a spare in one in my cupboard. I quickly checked the end of the hall, before ducking into my room and retrieving it. I threw it across to him and he promptly dropped it.

"Thanks," he said, picked it up and ran into his room to stick it into his webbing.

"Platoon Atten-shun!" commanded our Platoon Sergeant from the end of the hall.

Possum was still inside his room but there was nothing we could do about that now. In unison, we lifted our feet up to the regulation height and slammed them into the ground, careful to not scuff the polish off the inside of our heels as we did so. With our head and eyes to the front, those of us at the end of the hall struggled to make out who was standing next to the Platoon Sergeant.

"This morning's inspection is going to be conducted by the CSM," we were informed as the Platoon Sergeant looked down the hall. Noting the Possum was absent, she added, "We will start with your room, Rickson."

Hearing this the Possum quickly re-appeared outside his room, his face still flustered, but looking a bit more relieved. He gave me a thumbs-up and braced himself up beside his door.

As the CSM and Platoon Sergeant marched up the hall, I thought I knew what was in store for me. Best bet was that I'd end up with a couple of show parades, just to remind me that I was still on his shit list. That didn't bother me too much, as we were at the range for most of the week, so I'd have time to bog whatever it was he found during the inspection. The other alternative was that he'd just use the time to give me a solid chewing out and remind me to stop messing with the system. The trouble with getting in trouble a lot is that after a while it no longer means anything. The punishments all became different versions of the same theme, "just do what you're told, otherwise we are going to stuff you around". I knew this sort of thinking was exactly the sort of thing that got me into trouble in the first place, but I was never very good at turning the cynical part of my brain off. I was still of the belief that part of the reason we had passed selection was that we had demonstrated an ability to think. I agreed with the fact that rules and punishments were a necessary part of the Army, as they were for the rest of society, but I had this idea in my head that our time at the College was supposed to teach us more than just how to follow rules. After all, our instructors continuously reminded us that we were expected to think for ourselves and question things we felt were not right.

"Ahh Cadet Rickson, what a great way to start the week," the CSM said as he walked into my room. I followed him in as the Platoon Sergeant waited at the door holding her notebook.

He spent the next minute or so prodding and poking around my room. My rifle barrel was held up to the light to look for any stray specks of dust and the chinstrap on my hat peered into. I was surprised at his nonchalance, as I'd expected him to be a lot more thorough. After shutting the doors to my cupboards, he turned to face me.

"Cadet Rickson, your room is OK, however, your rifle needs work to remove the build-up around the bolt-face and your brass has scratches in it where you have not used the right cloth. Make time with your Platoon Sergeant to re-inspect them."

"Yes, CSM," I replied and looked straight ahead.

"Now, as you may know, the OC was in on Saturday after parade and had a look through the company leave book," he said, leaning on my desk, "your name has come up as not having signed back in after leave on Friday night. Do you know anything about this?"

"Yes CSM," I said, doing my best to keep my thoughts on the policing of the leave book and other similar rules to myself.

"So, you're aware of the fact that you did not sign back in on your return from leave on Friday night?"

"Yes CSM."

"And you are aware of the fact that you have to sign in and out, every time you go on leave, as per Corps standing orders?" he continued.

I paused for a minute, the logic cogs in my brain complaining loudly, as the enforcement of admin rules in my opinion should be an admin matter, not a disciplinary one. But I knew what was coming, so bit my tongue and answered curtly.

"Yes CSM, it won't happen again."

"It had better not, but in the interim, you've got a date with the Drilly this afternoon at 1630. I expect you're going to get charged as you've been on the round-about for too long now and you're due. So, I've got a bit of advice for you. Are you ready?" as he spoke, he turned around and was looking out of my window.

"Yes CSM, of course," I said, hoping my cynicism wasn't too obvious.

"First, don't be late to the Drilly's office this afternoon. Secondly, if you get charged, don't do anything stupid. No bullshit, just nod your head, plead guilty and take the punishment on the chin. Even though you and I don't get on, I think you've got what it takes to graduate, which means at some stage we will have to be in the same Army together. But only if you can pull your head in. That is all."

"Will do CSM, thanks," I replied.

For all my misgivings about the CSM, I had to admit it was good advice and I knew I should listen. With that he marched out into the corridor and I returned to my place outside my door. The Platoon Sergeant stood next to me as the CSM entered Possum's room and whispered, "We'll catch up about the inspections this afternoon after you've seen the Drilly. Come see me in my room before dinner and we'll have a chat."

At least I knew where I stood with the charge now and in some ways that was a bit of a relief, but it didn't mean the arse-chewing I was going to get from Sergeant Zimburger was going to be any more fun.

Knowing what was coming, I could at least make sure I turned up in the right frame of mine. At the end of the inspections, the platoon was given a quick debrief by the CSM, who reminded us that we needed to be able to see our teeth in our chinstraps, our brass and parade boots. The horizontal surfaces should be clean enough to eat off and that we needed to do these things in order to set an example for our troops. After handing back to the Platoon Sergeant, the CSM disappeared down the stairs and we were dismissed. We scrambled back into our rooms to re-assemble our rifles so they could be secured, but the rest of our kit was left where it was. Given we'd already just been through an inspection this morning, it was pretty much guaranteed that there wouldn't be any surprise room visits today. I grabbed my peaked cap, armed myself with my books and punched out of the lines to join up with the rest of my classmates as they headed for the lecture rooms.

The rest of the day was filled with tactics, service writing and PT lessons. We learned that most of us had got through our first TEWT, with only a couple of cadets up for re-tests. Service writing was painful as usual, as we spent the whole double period learning to compose letters using the Army standards for placement, spacing, lettering etc. This was still done by hand on ruled Army issued paper, which still blew my mind as even the most basic government offices were filled with computers. But that was the way we were expected to learn, so that was what we did. The PT session was punishing as usual, with the PTI's deciding that today would be a great day to work on our endurance. We spent the better part of two hours running laps around the football fields carrying various heavy objects in teams and doing as many push-ups as we could. Army PT may have looked straight forward, but it was never easy. The PTI's could never be accused of lacking imagination when it came to finding different ways to lift, carry and drag the arsenal of boxes, ropes and steel bars they had stashed in the sheds behind the gym. By the time we finally made it back to the gym, my fatigues were dripping with sweat and all I wanted to do was lie down under a cool shower.

"I don't know about you blokes, but that almost killed me. I think my fitness is going backwards," Watts spluttered on the run back to the lines.

"You'll be right mate. Remember, what doesn't kill us only makes us stronger," offered Walker as he bounded along beside me.

"In which case you can carry me for the next session. It'll do wonders for your fitness," Watts fired back.

"But it might also kill you too," I said with a sly grin.

As the rest of the company headed back to their rooms when we got back to the company, I headed down to Sergeant Zimburgers office. As expected, he was sitting in his office, plunking away on his issued computer. I knocked on the door and peered in, "You wanted to see me Sergeant Zimburger?"

"Wait," came the curt reply and I could hear him shuffling papers around on his desk.

"Cadet Rickson come on in," he said after a moment.

I marched in and stood to attention in front of his desk. By now I had the drill down pat, and knew I was standing dead center of the red X he had marked on his floor. I could see him looking over his desk to check I was on the right spot before he started.

"Do you know why you are here?"

I knew this wasn't an existential question, but every time I heard one of the DS say it, I was tempted to start explaining my thoughts about life, the universe and everything. However, I knew the answer he was after and the words of Sergeant Ruth still echoed in my head after our exchange at the rugby oval.

"Yes, Sergeant."

"And why is that?" he asked, obviously unimpressed by the fact that I hadn't already dobbed myself in.

"The CSM said you wanted to see me because I didn't sign the leave book on Friday night."

"Correct. Are you aware of the fact that whenever you go on leave you are to sign out and then back in in the company leave book?"

"Yes, Sergeant."

"Signing the company leave book is important, so that we know who is on barracks at any time and is stipulated in the Corps Standing Orders, which makes it a lawful order. You have now disobeyed a lawful general order and as such are going to be charged under Section 27 of the DFDA. Do you understand?" he said with a smile as he produced an Army PD-105 form, or charge sheet as we knew them.

"Yes, Sergeant," I replied keeping my head and eyes fixed on the wall above his desk.

"Now, you are going to need to find yourself a defending officer. I recommend you speak to your Platoon Sergeant and see if she can help as she is pretty squared away. The charge is going to be held on Friday at 1000 hours in the CO's office. In between now and then, you need to go through the charge sheet, confirm your details are correct and get back to me with your defending officer's name. Understood?"

"Yes, Sergeant."

"Now, this isn't the first time you've been in my office and I'm guessing it won't be the last. But I have been known to be wrong before and I'd be much happier if you just squared yourself away and got off the roundabout so I could spend my time doing something else instead of filling out charge sheets for you. As a young officer, it behoves you to follow orders and set an example for your troops. Following orders is pretty simple and I'd expect even you could do it if you set your mind to it. Any questions?"

"No, Sergeant."

"Now, one last thing," he added and looked at me through his squinted eyes, "Do not attempt to plead not guilty to this charge. The evidence is clear, you have broken the rules, so you are going to be charged and you are going to be guilty. Fill out the forms, following the bouncing ball and do your time. Do those things and then keep your nose clear for the next month and you may just get off my shit list. That is all."

"Yes, Sergeant."

I braced up, turned and marched out with the charge sheet tucked under one arm and my other arm punching through to shoulder height. That wasn't as bad as I thought it could have been, I thought and strolled back to the platoon. Remembering her words after parade, I headed to the Platoon Sergeants room first. I knocked on the door and waited.

"Who is it?" she asked.

"Just me, back from the Drilly," I said and leant against the wall.

"How did you go?" she asked as she opened the door.

"As expected," I replied and held up the PD-105.

"Seen... Why don't you come in and have a seat," she said and motioned me into her room before propping the door open. The rules stipulated that a cadet wasn't officially allowed to be in another cadet's room without the door open. The Platoon Sergeant's rooms were at the end of the hall in Long Tan company and were much bigger than the other rooms. They would have been a pain in the backside to clean if you were in 2nd or 3rd class, but the inspections of the Platoon Sergeant's rooms were usually no more than a cursory glance. There was a set of couches in the middle of the room and she pointed me in their direction.

"Right, give us a look at the charge sheet then," she said and took a seat at her desk.

I handed it over and plonked down on one of the worn couches that were obviously Army issue. They were put together with a series of bent steel tubes and hard-wearing cushions that had been worn thin from years of cadet use. As I waited for her to finish reading the charge sheet, I glanced around the room. Except for what looked like a couple of small family photos, the room was bereft of any personality. It felt bare and cold and I wondered how she survived without in the very least a couple of books.

"Well, this is pretty straight forward. Do you know what you need to do from here?" she asked and placed the paperwork on the table.

"I do," I said with a smile.

She looked puzzled and drew her eyebrows together.

"Why am I not surprised… do you need someone to be defending officer for you?"

"All good. One of the cadets from Kokoda is going to do it for me," I replied with a smile.

She shook her head.

"Look, I know you have trouble dealing with authority and I know you don't care much about getting advice from me, but do not screw around with this. This is going to be heard by the CO and he is the last person you want to mess around with. Remember, you got caught, so you're guilty and that's the way you play it," she said and shook her head again.

"All good. I'll keep it simple," I replied with a smile.

"Now when did you want to have a look at my brass and rifle? Best we get that done before I'm back on the square again I reckon." "Bring them in tomorrow after dinner," she said and sighed.

"Ripper, I'll see you then, then. Thanks for the chat," I said, grabbed the charge sheets and headed back down the hall.

As I approached my room, I noticed the corner of an envelope sticking out from under the door. It looked like standard Army stationery and I wondered what new trouble I could have managed to get into since leaving the Drilly's office. In my head, I went through the last few days, trying to figure out what I might have done that might have resulted in another visit from the DS. I slipped my key in the door and reached down for the envelope. On the front it read:

Cadet Rickson, Long Tan Company
RMC, Canberra

I kicked my door closed behind me and lay back on my bed. I ripped the envelope open and emptied the contents. To my surprise, it contained a tattered beer coaster and a handwritten letter. The coaster was from some dodgy pub in Townsville and the letter was from one of my mates who had graduated the year before.

Hey Matey,

Was out with the boys last weekend and they were asking after you. We were taking bets as to how many extra's we reckon you've done by now. I've got you down for twenty, let me know if you've beaten that yet.

Things up here are tops. I'm still running around like a chook with my head off most days and my OC is a pain in the date. But we've got a decent bunch of blokes up here and the night life is bloody awesome. As you can imagine the Townsville girls love me!

Anyway, just wanted to check in and tell you to keep at it. I know I hated 2nd class, but I somehow, I got through so there is hope for you yet!

Giddy up,

VB

I looked at the coaster in my other hand. It was covered in smudged signatures and dodgy sketches of male appendages. I leaned back against the wall and grinned. Maybe there was a light at the end of the tunnel, I thought. If those blokes had managed to make it through in one piece, then there was no reason I couldn't do the same.

Tuesday morning kicked off without much fuss. After morning parade, we had drill and then a double session of PT. After PT, most of us were famished, so we loaded up our plates up at lunch before heading back to the lecture hall for the afternoon session. The afternoon sessions were normally tough, and even more so after loading ourselves up with mess food at lunch. As the lesson wore on the combination of a heavy lunch and a darkened classroom went to work. If we felt drowsy, the recommended practice was to stand up and take notes from the aisles to save receiving a spray from the instructor. But try as we might, the 'rack monster' still managed to claim a few victims as the lesson wore on and the weariness took its toll. This never escaped the watchful eye of the instructors and the lesson quickly ground to a halt if they saw someone's head start to roll. By mid-way point of the lesson, I looked around the room to see a handful of my classmates standing.

In the center of the room, Captain Schwartz walked us through the importance of being able to think on the move and how to control our platoon on the battlefield. Between slides, he would stop and check we were paying attention.

"Right, any questions so far?" he said, looking up from the lectern.

The room was silent, so he turned back to the screen.

"I might have something to add, if you don't mind Captain Schwartz?" a voice offered from the shadows.

Unbeknown to us, the Commandant had crept into the lecture hall and had been silently listening in. Even though he was a big man, he could still move quietly and had even been known to slip on the rugby boots from time to time. He had served in Vietnam and bore a number of decorations for his service, which automatically earned our respect. To boot, he rarely saw the need to raise his voice as his presence alone was enough to silence the room. When he talked, we listened.

"Class!" said Captain Schwartz and we braced up in our chairs.

"At ease," the Commandant replied and took up a position in the middle of the room.

Illuminated by the warm glow of the downlights, he surveyed the imaginary battlefield laid out around him and smiled.

"Now, as you know I was in your position once," he said, looking around the room. We sat in awe; you could have quite literally heard a pin drop in the hall.

"And after I graduated, I was lucky enough to be sent to Vietnam to put my skills to the test. As a young platoon commander, I thought I knew my stuff. But more importantly, I thought I knew my men."

He spoke with a reverence for the men he had served with and imparted to us the importance of not only mastering tactics, but also in learning to understand the soldiers we served with. Without them, we were simply young officers with a headful of knowledge, but with them and alongside them, we were a formidable force that was capable of amazing things. He finished with a smile and looked around the room to make sure we were listening, before handing back to Captain Schwartz and disappearing into the darkness.

Like many a soldier or young officer before us, we were in awe of the stories told by veterans of previous conflicts and wars. Each of us knew the details of at least one particular war or battle by heart, as they formed part of our own story and our own motivation for joining. Whether it was because of a relative who fought on the Somme, in the Pacific, in Vietnam, or someone in between. We all held some concept of what war was like and in our own way looked forward to the day we could test ourselves on a battlefield of our own. Whether we wanted to be laying ambushes at night in the jungle or calling in fire missions from a hilltop in some far away land, we longed for war stories of our own that we could talk about one day.

After dinner that night, I lay in my bed thinking about the Commandant's experience and wondered where my own path would take me. The old great enemies had long since fallen, there were no more Nazi's, no Japanese Empire and even the Russians had all but shut-up shop. The Cold War no longer bubbled away on the borders of Europe and the threat of nuclear destruction was no more than a whisper. The last big dust-up in the Gulf was long gone and even Africa seemed to be relatively stable. Of course, there were still a handful of madmen in charge of countries around the world, but on the whole the chances of Australian forces being deployed again on active duty appeared slim. In our spare time, we'd discuss who we thought might have a shot at Special Forces after graduation, or a gig on a UN Peace Keeping mission, or maybe even a cushy exchange to the UK or USA. Like it or not, periods of peace were unsettling for young minds who were being trained for war. As young leaders we knew that the devil would find work for idle hands, so we could expect to spend much of our time doing administrative tasks and managing soldiers who inevitably found ways to get into trouble if they were in barracks for too long. Give me a posting where I could spend 6-months a year in the field, I thought. That would keep us busy, reduce the admin and keep us focused on staying sharp.

I spent that night and any spare time I had the next few days, preparing for the charge on Friday. Even though it was daunting, I realized it was all just a part of the game and in the long run I'd survive. Just like the challenges we faced each week; I knew I'd get through it and knew there were plenty more challenges like it to come. If nothing else, our training taught us that the human mind adapts to new situations fast, even when things seem scary, insurmountable or impossible. For better or worse, the discipline system was no different. It was meant to scare the shit out of you, but it was just another challenge that we had to go through. After all, they couldn't take my birthday off me, I reminded myself with a grin.

The rest of the week flew by and before I had time to think about it, I was throwing on a fresh uniform and heading down to the CO's office. I met KD outside the headquarters building at 1545 and we waited for the RSM to call us inside.

"Nervous?" he asked.

"Nah," I replied foolishly, knowing what we were about to do.

"You sure you want to use our defense statement?" he enquired.

"In for a penny, in for a pounding. I'm getting my arse kicked either way, so we may as well have a go at telling the truth. It'll make for a good story one of these days," I said with a grin.

"Righto, you two. Get in here," yelled the RSM from inside the building.

The RSM stood inside the door, pace-stick firmly tucked under one arm. We marched in and halted in the hall outside the CO's office.

"Cadet Rickson are you aware of how this works?" he said in his usual gravelly voice.

"Yes, Sir," I replied crisply.

Inside the court, the CO sat at his desk with two other cadets, one seated and one standing. The one standing was the Prosecutor, the one sitting was the Scribe. For any charges whilst we were at the College, unless they were of a significant nature, the practice was to also use the experience as a teaching one and so other cadets were required to fill the other key roles in the court. The RSM ushered KD in to join them.

"RSM. March in the accused," the CO ordered from behind his desk and off we went.

"Cadet Rickson, quick... march!" said the RSM behind me and followed me in.

"Mark time," he called when I was in the middle of the room, followed by, "Halt!" when he had entered the room and pulled the door closed behind him.

I stood looking straight ahead, thumbs pressing onto the top of my clenched fists, head high and heart racing. No matter how many times I did this, the gravity of the occasion still got the adrenaline going.

"Prosecutor read the charge," the CO said.

Drawing up the PD-105, the Prosecutor proceeded to read out my crime and the evidence that guaranteed my guilt.

"Cadet Rickson, you are hereby charged under section..." as he read the charge, my mind wandered. I wondered why there was always a portrait of the Queen behind the CO's desk and why it was that particular one. Surely, she had aged a bit since then, maybe they should have a more recent one, I thought.

"Thank you, Prosecutor," said the CO, snapping me back into reality.

The RSM handed the PD-105 to the CO, who examined it thoroughly. I wondered what he was looking for, as it had been meticulously checked and double-checked before it had got to him.

"Cadet Rickson, how do you plead?" he said, looking directly at me.

"Guilty, Sir," I replied.

"Scribe, note that the accused has entered a plea of guilty," he said and looked over to the Scribe, who scribbled away furiously.

"Cadet Rickson, I hereby find you guilty of disobeying a lawful general order. Do you wish to have anyone speak in your defense?"

"Yes Sir, I wish to have Cadet Davidson speak on my behalf," I replied.

"Cadet Davidson, please read your statement," the CO said and sat back in his chair.

This was usually the bit where the defending officer read one of those flattering statements about what a good cadet you were, outlined your academic record and said that you were committed to a long career in the Army. On occasion, written statements from senior cadets or friendly instructors were tendered to support your case. None of these mattered of course, as the judge had always made their mind up before you went in. We knew the extent of punishments available for each offence, as they were laid out in the Defence Force Discipline Act we that we been taught about. I knew the scale of punishments better than most, as well as what the CO had given out previously through the rumor-mill. I also knew that my OC would have certainly had a word to the CO before the charge and would have recommended throwing the book at me, so I knew what was coming. As to whether that made my defense any more sensible was debatable.

KD shuffled his papers, looked at me briefly and proceeded to read out our agreed statement.

"Sir, I would like to make the following statement on behalf of the accused," he started.

"No longer 'accused', Cadet Davidson, he is now guilty," corrected the RSM.

"Yes, Sir. I would now like to make the following statement on behalf of the guilty party. Cadet Rickson acknowledges the fact that he did not sign into the leave book upon return from leave, however, he would like to point out the fact that he was actually back from leave and was going to sign the leave book when it was inspected by the OC. He would also like to note that it is common practice for many cadets not to sign the leave book, with a view to avoiding the need to sign back in when they return late in the evenings from leave.

As such, he would like it noted that..."

"Stop!" the CO ordered and visibly stiffened in his chair.

"Cadet Davidson, are you telling me that in mitigation of his guilt, Cadet Rickson is telling me other cadets do not follow standing orders? Which are in fact, my orders?" he fumed.

The room went silent as the CO contemplated his next move.

"RSM, march out the guilty party," he said, turning to the RSM. The Prosecutor and Scribe, without any guidance, simply braced up and looked bewildered.

"Cadet Rickson, about turn. Quick march," the RSM barked and off I went.

"Right, turn," he said as I reached the hallway, only a couple of steps behind me. "Left, right, left, right, left," he barked as I marched onward, destination unknown.

"Mark time," he said as I reached the door to his office. He pushed the door open, before marching me into his office. I marked time in the middle of his office while he walked around behind his desk and sat in his chair.

"Halt!" he ordered, "Cadet Davidson, get in here too."

KD marched in and halted beside me. Standing side by side, I imagined that this was what it would have been like to be at the wrong end of a firing party. He paused and sat back in his chair. Silence hung in the air.

"Cadets, you should know a lot better than this," he began calmly and turned to his bookshelf.

It was filled with the numerous pams necessary to make the College run smoothly, military history books, personal memorabilia and plaques he had received from the units he'd served at. It was part war memorial and part library. He reached for one of the small green books that was about a finger width thick and placed it on the desk in front of him.

"Do you gentlemen recognize this book?" he asked.

"Yes, Sir," we answered in unison before even seeing it.

The book was a drab colored paperback with the words, "Junior Leadership on the Battlefield" printed across the cover. It was one of the books each of us had been issued and we were expected to know it inside out and back to front.

"I suggest you both take the time to re-read this book. As junior officers, you will be leaders. As such, you do not have a choice of which orders you follow, and nor do you expect your soldiers to choose. Standing orders are the orders of the Commanding Officer. As a junior officer it is your job to follow them and enforce them, not to question them and undermine the authority of the CO," he said, looking us with a steely gaze.

"Are you picking up what I am putting down, gentlemen?"

"Yes, Sir," we answered again. This was no two-way conversation, he was on 'send' and we were on 'receive'. When the RSM spoke, we listened, as his words contained wisdom gained over many years of soldiering. Even though he rarely lost his temper and often had a wry smile on his face, none of us ever thought of trying to cross him.

"Righto, then. Here's what is going to happen. I am going to march you back into the CO's office. You are not going to submit a statement in your defense. Instead, you are going to accept your punishment, and that is going to be that. Is that clear gentlemen?"

"Yes, Sir," we replied in unison.

And so, that was what we did. We marched back down the hall and into the CO's office again. The CO was still in his chair and the other cadets looked like they hadn't moved. I wondered if they had been let go or whether they'd stayed in place the whole time. It was as likely they hadn't and they both looked confused as to what was going on. The RSM handed back over to the CO and we did as we were told. The CO gave us another arse kicking and left us in no doubt as to where we stood. I was also reminded that I was on very, very thin ice from here on. One slip up and there was no way I was graduating.

Due to our performance, I ended up with fourteen days on the square, twenty-one days confined to barracks and got docked three days' pay. Whilst the first part of the punishment would be a pain in the backside, he last bit really stung.

"Well, that did not go quite as we planned it," I said to KD as we marched back to the lines.

"Could have been worse. You've still got your birthday... but only just," he replied with his usual cheeky grin.

We parted ways at the top of the parade ground, and he headed up the hill to Kokoda while I kept marching towards Long Tan. On the way back, I saluted the memorial and wondered how many of the cadets whose names were on memorial had ended up in the CO's office when they'd been at the College. While the world had changed plenty since the College was founded, I didn't doubt that plenty of my predecessors had also spent a bit of time on the square during their time in training. Looking across at the parade ground, I tried to imagine what it would have been like to be march the square fifty years ago. I imagined what it would have been like trying to get through a Canberra winter if all you had to keep you warm was a cotton shirt and wool overcoat. Hell, if they could do their time and make it through, so could I, I thought and grinned.

My first full day of punishments started the next day, so I spent the rest of the evening making sure my gear was in order and checking what times each of the parades were. Those on restriction of privileges (ROPs) started their day at 0630 with a drill parade. Whilst normal drill was done in fatigues and rifle, for ROPs you were required to wear your full field gear, including webbing, pack and rifle. It all had to be packed as per the field pam and just to make sure, the Duty Officer's first job after calling the roll was to conduct an inspection of your gear to make sure you had everything. This consisted of the Duty Officer asking you to present a number of randomly chosen items, which you held above your head to prove that you had them. Water bottles were checked to ensure they were full, and the inside of the pack inspected to make sure you didn't have a pillow in place of your full issue of field gear. After the gear check, the next forty-five minutes was spent doing drill on the square. Wearing all the extra gear, drill was tiring and sucked even more than it did usually, which was the point. You got let off with minimal time to spare, so you had to bolt back to your lines in order to be ready for the morning's first parade. The rest of the day was as normal until 1700, when you repeated the exercise again. ROPs also included two check parades after dinner, to make sure you were still in the barracks. On top of your normal daily load, ROPs were a pain in the arse, but they were a good lesson in time management.

Besides the early start and extra dick around on BC days, ROPs never bothered me that much. Like most of my classmates, any spare time that wasn't already allocated to lessons or used preparing for tests was usually wasted lying in our farter or sitting around drinking brews. During the first week, your mates were there to help you out, always checking you were on time and that you had all of your gear. When you were short any issued field gear, they leant you theirs. If you needed a hand getting other work done, they'd also help out. Whilst the punishment was meant to teach you a lesson and remind you to follow the rules, in many ways it also cemented the friendships you had.

As I sat preparing my gear for the first drill parade that night, Hobbes dropped in to make sure I had all the gear I was supposed to be carrying.

"Pan set messing?" he said.

I held up the folding set of eating utensils we were issued to eat out of but never carried.

"Check," I'd reply and stuff them back in my pack.

"Millbank filter, by one."

"Check."

"Cups canteen?"

"Check."

When we found something missing, we'd find a spare one somewhere and chuck it in. We sipped the remnants of ration pack coffee and laughed at the absurdity of it all. I knew that whilst it was a dick-around for him to be lending me a hand, he was happy to help. I knew, he was also happy that it wasn't him.

The next two weeks rolled by pretty quick. The tactics lessons and TEWTS kept us on our toes, whilst the service writing bored us to tears. PT still brought plenty of sweat but also plenty of laughs. I was pissed-off to miss the trip to the rugby game at Jindabyne, but there was nothing I could do about it. As the days were already getting colder, the morning parades were often held on a misty parade ground. After the first few days, I settled into a routine and the days seemed to fly by.

Most of the days I was the only one on the parade ground, which must have looked pretty hilarious for anyone watching. A few of the Duty Officers ran out of new drill commands after about ten minutes, as they weren't used to giving drill commands without a parade and the orders were to give the 'roppers' a new command every five to ten steps. I quietly chuckled when the foreign cadets were Duty Officer as their English wasn't always that clear and their knowledge of drill commands was also a bit fuzzy. One morning, in heavy fog, I ignored the drill commands and made up my own, eventually ending up at the far end of the parade ground. Through the mist, I could hear the Duty Officer barking orders as I executed my own movements. After forty-five mins of walking around in circles I marched myself back to the top of the parade ground and was dismissed by a puzzled PNG cadet. Luckily, he didn't take it personally.

On the final day of ROP's, a few of my mates had arranged to sit in one of the rooms in Alamein company that fronted the drill square and they clapped me off as I was dismissed from my final parade. Like some sort of miniature version of graduation parade, I tossed my hat into the air and high fived the air about me. The Duty Officer even managed to crack a smile, before reminding me to put my hat back on and stop screwing-around. I still had seven days of stoppage of leave to go, but this was nothing after the two weeks of ROPS. Coincidentally, the Duty Officer on my final day was cadet Woods and he grinned when he saw me.

"Still here?" he asked at the morning parade.

"Last day," I smiled back.

"About time," he replied with a knowing look.

After being dismissed at the last parade of the night, he pulled me aside once all of the other cadets were gone.

"Oi, Rickson. Get over here," he said.

We walked around to the back of Alamein company where we could chat out of sight from the rest of the Corps.

"Good to see you're finally off the round-about," he said, removing his hat.

"Yeah, me too," I replied.

"Now, what're the chances you can get yourself off the numerous shit-lists you're on and get on with it?" he said and crossed his arms.

"Better than average," I said with a smile.

He looked at me and his smile faded.

"Well listen up for the next minute. From all accounts, you're not a bad bloke, but you have a nasty habit of fucking up. Quite often, it seems, just for the sake of it. Plenty of cadets have been given the boot for less, so I don't know how you have made it this far. But you have, so don't bloody waste it. Get through this place and maybe, just maybe, one of these days, I'll buy you a beer. Got me?" he finished by giving me a quick prod in the chest with one of his massive fingers.

I braced up and nodded. Usually, a bumph from one of the senior class would go straight over my head, but for once I listened. He wasn't kicking my ass just to prove he was six months ahead of me, he actually seemed to give a shit. Coming from someone who had seen plenty of trouble themselves, I figured he was talking from experience.

"Loud and clear," I replied and for once, I think I meant it.

On the way back to the company, I felt relieved and like a weight had been lifted off my shoulders. I no longer felt like I needed to fight the system. I realized that getting through the College was only the beginning of what I'd signed up for. I smiled as I pushed my way through the front doors of the company and was still smiling when my classmate turned up with a bottle of port to celebrate. You never quite appreciate how many hours there are in a day and how many of them you waste doing not much in particular, until you've had every one of them planned for you. That night I had the best sleep I'd ever had and knew exactly why.

The next week was going to be spent on the rifle range working on our shooting skills with the F-89 Minimi or 'gun' as we knew it. Whilst we were already familiar with the gun from our field exercises, most of our time carrying them around only involved firing blanks, so any opportunity to fire live ammunition was something to look forward to. As officers, we weren't expected to carry or fire the gun, but it was an essential tool in the tactical toolkit of a junior officer, so we were expected to master its application. Range days were pretty much like a day off compared to anything else we did. Besides a couple of series of drills prior to shooting to make sure we could handle the weapon safely, the bulk of the day was spent waiting around, shooting or patching out targets.

Once onboard the buses, we bundled into the seats, making sure we were sitting next to our mates so we could continue the conversations we'd had over breakfast. We joked about the antics we'd seen at BC Day, the bumphings that we'd heard recently and any particularly good gossip that might be of use in preparing for our next TEWT. Arriving at the range, we pulled our gear and guns off the buses before marching up to the range. From there we were split into groups (serials) and given the order in which we'd be shooting for the day. As we were using the old manual range, one of the groups would be responsible for looking after the targets during each serial, on what we called 'butts party".

Our serial was called up to collect weapons and head over to a shady spot for a bit of refresher training. In the field the gun was a two-man operation, with the gunner and number two working together to provide fire support for the rest of the section. On the range, we handled the gun by ourselves, which was no trouble for most cadets, but often caused a few issues for the girls or smaller guys. Particularly if you had to do a barrel change when the thing was hot. So, we always kicked off any session at the range with a revision on the safe handling of the weapon, followed by stoppage drills and usually a barrel change or two thrown in for good measure. The group I was in had drawn Sergeant Ruth as our instructor, which promised to be entertaining as he loved gun drills. The Army has a habit of getting the bigger guys in a unit to carry all the heavy stuff, which often included the gun, particularly as the previous generation of machine guns were heavy bloody things. From the tales we were told, if you got stuck patrolling for a few weeks carrying the old M-60, you would have given your left nut (or something of equivalent value for female cadets) to swap for one of our modern weapons. Based on his size, it was pretty obvious that in his early days as an infantry soldier, Sergeant Ruth had spent plenty of time carrying the gun for his section and had come to love it. He was passionate about the way we trained, and he approached the task much the same way he did a game of rugby. Instead of the dry staccato we were blasted with on the drill square, he delivered his commands the same way that a team captain would deliver a pre-game speech.

For the next thirty minutes we repeatedly practiced clearing feed chambers, changing magazines, fixing gas settings and changing barrels until he was satisfied, we would be safe on the range. We hoped that we would be accurate as well, but that came down to our own skill and application of the marksmanship principals that had been drilled into us. The gun was a different beast to our standard rifles and had to be handled carefully if you didn't want to see your rounds drift over the top of the target to create little puffs of dust on at the end of the range. As we'd find out when it was our turn on the mound, you needed a combination of care and determination to get the gun to deliver an accurate stream of fire onto your target.

After handing our guns over to the next serial, we were given five minutes to grab a brew and whatever snacks the mess staff had boxed up for us. This usually consisted of individually wrapped biscuits or fruit cake, which were consumed with instant coffee or weak cordial. Amongst cadets, fruit cake was known as 'fart cake' for the obvious reasons and you could be guaranteed it would deliver noisy consequences on the bus ride home. I pulled up a spot on the bench next to the Cobbler to ask him about his BC day.

"Hey mate, I heard you've had a good morning," I said.

"Fuck yeah, had a bloody shocker at this morning's inspection. Who told you?" he laughed.

I flicked a thumb over at the group of cadets from his company who were lounging around at the other side of the shed.

"Figures," was his reply and he took a swig from his mug.

College Blues

"I hear you're in worse shit than me though," he added.

"Not anymore. I finished my last days on the square last Friday. Now all I've got to do is keep my nose clean until 1st class graduate," I replied.

"What do you reckon the chances of that are?" he asked.

"Better than average, but I've been wrong in the past," I said with a grin.

Sergeant Ruth appeared out the front of the shed.

"Serial 4, grab your gear and let's go. You're up next, go get your ammo and form up behind the mound."

With that, we knocked back the last of our brews, stuffed a couple of extra biscuits into our pockets and headed off.

We collected our ammunition from the makeshift armoury that was set up in one of the training sheds and plodded back to the firing mound. As we approached, we heard the 'rat-tat-tat' of the guns on the mound being fired. After the last rounds were fired, we could hear the guns being cocked simultaneously, so the weapons could be cleared by the instructors. We could hear the instructors yell "clear!" as they inspecting each weapon. Next came the dry-clicking sound of the feed-trays being closed and the actions being fired. We saw the red range flag come down at both ends of the range as the all clear was given and the serials changed over.

"Serial 4, get up here," the range OC, Sergeant England yelled.

We stepped up to the mound and covered off each of the lanes to wait for the serial to commence. At the other end of the range the butts party walked out from behind the protection of the mound and towards the firing mound. As the groups approached the half-way mark, Sergeant England yelled, "We haven't got all bloody day, move with a sense of purpose!"

Both parties responded by shuffling a bit quicker until the serial before us was well hidden behind the mound where the targets were housed, and the other serial was well past the firing point. The red flags were raised again to let us know that live firing could commence.

"Righto you lot, cover off on your lane and number off from the left!" Sergeant England yelled.

"One!" the cadets at both ends of the serial simultaneously yelled, before one of the other cadets continued, "Two?"

"Stop, stop, stop!!!" Sergeant England screamed and turned to the cadet at the right end of the mound.

"Hey, you. Numb nuts at the far-right end. What's your name?"

"Cadet George," replied the offender.

"Are you at the left end of the serial?" the Sergeant England yelled, his face starting to go slightly red.

"No, Sergeant," George replied.

"Good, now we're all squared away with our left and rights, let's try it again. Cover off on your lane and number off from the left!"

We got it right the next time and he proceeded with the brief. He reminded us of what was required, which would involve shooting short bursts at targets at 100-meters. For most of us, this was the sort of thing we had joined the Army for, and we were pumped to be firing live rounds instead of blanks for a change. Our serial got through without many stuff ups, although the bloke next to me managed to catch a handful of hot shell cases on his back and burst out swearing mid-way through the serial. As he tried to brush the hot shells away, the instructor behind him used a well-placed boot and couple of words of encouragement to remind them to keep his barrel pointed down range. At the end of the serial, we cleared the weapons and left them on the mound to change over with the butts party, this time making sure we got a hustle on to avoid incurring Sergeant England's wrath.

Marching down the dirt road towards the targets, our feet kicked up small puffs of red dust that hung in the air and caught the sunlight. Around us, the air was heavy with the smell of gunpowder and I was reminded of the Army that I'd seen in the brochures at recruiting. If only it could have been possible to spend most of our days at the range and in the field, I thought I would have been a much better cadet.

Most of the crap that normally got me into trouble didn't happen in the field, as this was where things made more sense to me. Sure, I would have missed going to the Moose and wasn't a fan of spending days in wet boots, but I reckon it would have been a fair trade.

Arriving at the targets, we bumped into one of the Corporals at field training wing who usually played enemy during our field exercises. When the rest of the field instructors were tied up with weapons training, they often roped in one of the enemy platoon section commanders to help out at the range.

"Righto you lot, you know the drill. Make sure the targets are all patched out properly and you record the scores correctly," he said casually.

"I'll give you the heads-up when they're about to start and then listen for my command for before putting them up. As soon as I give the 'targets down', make sure they come straight down. Don't fuck around or we'll screw up the timing for the next detail."

"Excuse me Corporal," a voice asked from the bay next to mine.

"Yeah, what is it?" Corporal Pagan replied.

"Are we allowed to smoke down here today?" Mick asked, holding up a pack of Winfield Blues.

"Sure, I don't see why not. But make sure you bin your butts and don't miss any of the serials," he said and reached for the handset of the radio beside him, waiting for the command to start.

We double checked each of the targets to make sure the serial before us had done their job. The targets were mounted with two wooden poles on each side that clipped into a sliding mechanism that allowed them to be raised and lowered above the mound overhead. This old-fashioned mechanism needed to be operated manually and hence, each serial required a butts party to operate the targets and count the holes in each target before patching them out with small black stick-on dots. We checked each target carefully, not wanting to give the cadet shooting at our target the chance of a few extra rounds on target due to us missing holes from previous serial. There was nothing worse than being beaten by someone who couldn't shoot straight because someone had stuffed up their scoring, either by accident or on purpose. The acrid smell of cigarette smoke wafted around us as we sat on the concrete wall and waited for the initial command to get the targets-up.

The static on the radio was replaced by Sergeant England's voice and Corporal Pagan gave us the order to stand-by. For the next half-an hour, we threw the targets up and down in a frenzy, echoing the commands of Corporal Pagan as he listened for his orders from the firing mound. We shared any biscuits we'd pinched and laughed any time one of us was late getting our target into the right position. Michaels was next to me and we pushed each other to be the fastest ones to get our targets up each time, throwing digs at each other whenever we won or lost.

"Too slow again Rickson, you'll need retraining I reckon," he'd yell as we reefed the targets down.

"You've got nothing Mick, I'm all over you," I'd yell in reply.

"Corporal, hey Corporal, this bloke is all over the show. Can you keep him down here all afternoon, I reckon he's a bit slow!" he yelled, a cigarette hanging out of the side of his mouth.

Even though no one ever got any awards for doing their job in the butts party, most of us thought it was a pretty good gig. You were out of the eyesight of the DS and as long as you didn't fuck up too badly, you could enjoy a bit of a laugh with your mates. In my opinion it was one of the better ways to spend an afternoon.

Once the last rounds were fired, we patched the targets up, counted up bullet holes and handed the score cards to Corporal Pagan, who sent us on our way back to the firing mound. As we walked back, Mick and I discussed life, rugby and how good it would be when we finally got our first postings. Like me, he loved his rugby, wasn't great in barracks and was always keen for a beer come Fridays. Unlike me, he was keen on going to infantry, which we were continuously told was the backbone of the Army. I still hadn't made my mind up and he poked me to come and join the real men in the infantry. At this stage of the training, most cadets had a pretty good idea of which Corps they wanted to go to and also had a pretty good idea of where they were in terms of performance, as this also played a big part in getting selected. As I would no longer be learning a trade as an armourer, I hadn't really made my mind up. Early on, I was thinking I'd have a shot at pilot training but was pretty certain that I was a long shot given my discipline record. My next choice was to wait and see how things went in 1st class, which was what I told him.

"Don't leave it to the last-minute mate," he reminded me, as we walked past the range flag, "you'll end up in Catering!"

"Could be worse, at least I'd be first to the bar on Fridays!" I replied.

"And Thursdays and Wednesdays," he added and we both grinned.

The last job of the day was to pick up the spent brass and link. We emu bobbed up and down the firing mound, tossing the brass and link into our bush hats. Picking up brass was a tedious job, but it gave you a pretty good idea of which cadets were apt to be jack as you could see how many times everyone emptied their bush hats. The jack cadets would walk up and down the mound numerous times, picking up a single round here or there, trying to look busy, whilst the rest of us approached it like a competition and scrambled to pick up as much as we could, knowing that the faster it was done, the faster we got home. Every now and then, one of the DS would notice one of the cadets doing their best to look busy and unload on them from atop the firing mound.

"Oi, numb nuts! Stop bludging and get to work!"

This would speed the process up as we tucked in to dig rounds out from under the grass and edges of the mound. Sergeant England walked around checking the job had been done properly, looking for any reflections that indicated brass may still be hiding somewhere.

Once he was satisfied that we were done, we assembled for a final range clearance to make sure no one might be trying to sneak out any live ammunition. We'd heard stories of cadets who had smuggled rounds out of range practices and snuck out with their rifles for a 'yippee shoot' in the hills around Canberra. As they would have been the only ones with fully automatic rifles, you could imagine it would have been pretty easy to hear and most of us thought these stories were no more than rumors.

"I have no live rounds or range produce in my possession Sir!" we yelled one after the other as the DS walked along each rank and checked our pouches.

On the bus on the way back, we discussed our shooting prowess, laughed at those who had caught a few hot rounds in their collars and joked about the numerous bumph's Sergeant England had handed out. On the whole, we agreed it had been a good day to be a cadet.

Arriving back at barracks, we sat in groups under the trees outside the armoury cleaning the guns. The guns weren't issued individually like our rifles, so we shared the cleaning duties for each gun between a handful of us. After stripping the gun down, we broke it down further into components and diligently cleaned each piece until it was free of carbon, dust and oil. A gun wouldn't be accepted back into the armoury until it was inspected by one of the DS and we knew there were very few shortcuts that could be taken if the gun was going to pass. We jammed our fingers into the breach with cleaning cloths, pulled through barrels, and wire brushed the various components that had been thoroughly covered in hardened carbon from the days shooting. At various stages of the process, we called the DS over to check each piece was done and discussed the best strategies to use to get into all of the hard-to-reach spots. The ex-soldiers usually knew a trick or two from their experience, so it was always good to have one of them in your group. We usually had Walker in our group and he always had a tip or two that helped, plus he loved his spare time more than most of us, so he was doubly motivated to get it done. Once all the guns were safely back in the armoury and all of the stores from the day handed back in, we were dismissed to head back to the lines.

"Good day, eh lads?" Watts said as we marched back to the company.

"Fucking good day," replied Hobbes, "If only we could spend half of every week on the range, this place would be awesome."

"Yeah, half on the range, half in the field and the other half in the Moose," I added with a grin.

"I reckon you'd spend three quarters in the Moose and the rest in the farter if you could," Hobbes said.

"I can't see that being a bad idea, I reckon I might just have a shot at graduating if that was the case!"

With the week on the range complete and our next set of TEWTS almost finished, we knew another field exercise wouldn't be far off. By now, our bodies had healed the cuts and bruises we'd picked up on the last exercise and to ensure we didn't get soft our program still had plenty of PT each week.

"Lean into it, let the hill do the work" Sergeant Tubbs reminded us as we double-timed up to the obstacle course.

As a warm-up for the obstacle course, the PTI's had decided that a quick jog around the College would be good for us. Dressed in fatigues, boots, webbing and rifles, we double-timed it past the lines and along the road that separated the College from the Defence Academy. As we sweated our way up the hill, we looked scornfully across at the Defence Academy cadets as they lounged around outside their buildings.

"Keep in-step you lot! Left, right, left, right, left, right, left!" Sergeant Tubbs yelled as he jogged along beside us.

I focused on keeping my steps in time with my classmates and leaned into hill. According to the PTI's, leaning into the hill was supposed to make it easier, but never noticed any difference.

After slogging our way up the final stages of the hill, we found ourselves at the obstacle course and prepared ourselves for the onslaught to come. With the sweat flowing freely, we were sorted out into teams and lined up at the start of the obstacle course. As we waited, we tightened our webbing straps and shortened our rifle sling lengths. Leaving your sling too long was a guaranteed way to get yourself a few extra bruises as you clambered over the obstacles only to have your rifle whip around and find a soft bit of your body to dig into. Not as bad, but equally as embarrassing was losing your rifle when your sling came undone on top of an obstacle. This guaranteed at least twenty push-ups along with the accompanying ribbing from the PTI's.

"Right! First group on my command, I want you to fly through this course at the speed of a thousand startled gazelles. On your mark", Sergeant Tubbs said theatrically and looked around to see if we were ready.

"Wait for it... Go!" he yelled, and the first group shot off.

Whether they managed to get moving at the speed of a thousand started gazelles was debatable. Our group was next in line and looking around at the rest of my team, I thought we were also pretty unlikely to make it to the designated speed. Most of our group were reasonably fit, but we had a couple of bigger units in there who would make the ropes and ten-foot wall a challenge.

"Next group ready. G! Wait for it..." Sergeant Tubbs barked, looking up and down the ranks

"Go!"

We bolted across to the start of the rope bridge and grabbed a hold of the hanging ropes. Pulling myself up to one of the dangling ropes, I curled the rope over one of my boots before dragging the loose rope back over the bridge of my foot. My hands climbed up the rope above me and pushed down on the rope with my other foot until I was in a semi-standing position. Army rope climbing was not pretty, but it was functional and if executed correctly would get you up to the rope bridge in three quick moves. The secret, we learned, was in being able to lock the rope in with your boots to take the stress out of your hands. Even though your field gear only added an extra five to ten kilos, it felt a hell of a lot more when you were trying to claw your way up two-inch hanging rope. At the top, I hung briefly before throwing my leg over the single strand rope bridge to finish lying on top of the rope. From there it was a delicate balancing act to pull yourself across the top of the rope until you hit the other end and climb down the hanging ropes without letting yourself fall.

I didn't mind rope climbing, even though it would always leave you with a handful of scrapes and bruises where the rope rubbed. As long as you worked on your technique you would get through. By going first, you also guaranteed yourself a breather while you waited for the rest of the section to get across. Given the group we had today, I knew that we'd be waiting for the couple of cadets in our team who were gravity challenged. The bigger blokes may have had an obvious advantage when it came to strength work, but the additional weight was not on their side when it came to climbing ropes or the numerous forms of chin-ups the PTIs had invented.

"Get your feet locked in cadet!" Tubbs offered as one of the bigger blokes in our group slid down the rope again.

Cadet Kew tipped the scales at a bit over a ton and was as strong as an ox, but gravity liked him too much to make rope climbing easy. He shook his hands to try and get the blood flowing before attempting the climb again. He almost made it to the top of the rope when his hands gave out on him and he plummeted to the ground with a thud.

"The rest of you get going," Tubbs yelled at us, looking down at Kew before adding, "You can drop and give me twenty and then get going with your mates. We will do some extra training later!"

Hauling our rifles off our shoulders, we charged towards the rest of the obstacles. We jumped over water filled pits, dodged around wooden barriers, leopard crawled under cargo nets and threw each other over the ten-foot wall. With his size, Kew was a good asset for the first part of the ten-foot wall and ended up almost throwing one of the girls right over the top. Even with two of us on the top of the wall, dragging him over the top took all of the strength we could muster.

"Jesus Kew, what have you been eating?" Hobbes quipped as we paused for a breath at the bottom of the wall.

"Little people like you and a bucketload of chicken gourmet," he replied with a grin.

We chuckled and hauled ourselves towards the rest of the obstacles. As I swung my body over the tower, I briefly caught a glimpse of the rest of our class as they clambered through the course behind us. Looking back at the mess of sweating bodies, I thought I could see a few smiles lurking behind the grimaces, before being reminded to get my arse moving again by the PTI below.

Jogging back to the lines, I could feel my muscles start to ache as the sweat ran down my back, but there was also a sensation of achievement that came with it. Back in the company, we sat around behind the building, stripped bare to the waist and with our rifles laid on top of our webbing. We shared cold cans of soft drink, compared bruises and discussed the best way to set up our webbing for future sessions. Finally, once we'd emptied our drinks, we'd haul ourselves off for a hot shower and whatever was to come next.

A couple of weeks later, we were back on the parade ground. With graduation parade for 1st class fast approaching, our days now included one if not two, extra sessions of drill to get us back up to parade standard. We practiced the march-on, the march past, hundreds of salutes, inspections and march-offs. As the week wore on, the clouds grew grey and the temperature kept falling. For the early morning sessions, we wore a thicker pair of socks and thermal underwear to avoid freezing while we waited for the inspection to finish. By the time we got back to the lines after the morning sessions, we often had to help each other to open the locks on our doors as our fingers were frozen into claws. On the day of the final parade, the weather gods turned against us and decided that they'd give us a proper demonstration of what Canberra winter looked like. As soon as we marched onto the parade ground the rain was horizontal and the wind felt like it had come straight off the top of Mount Kosciusko. We'd heard the weather forecast that morning and had rugged up as much as we could underneath our parade uniform.

"Isn't it supposed to mean you're going to war, if it rains on your grad parade?" Watts whispered as we completed our first lap of the march past.

"Dunno. All I do know is that we're going to have to do a hell of a lot of bogging to get these uniforms back up to spec," I replied.

At least the cold kept us focused and there was less of a chance of anyone baconing whilst we waited for the inspection to finish. By the time the senior class were dismissed, I was saturated to the bone and my feet felt as if I was standing in a bucket of icy water. I wriggled my toes and tensed my legs to keep the blood flowing. It didn't seem to help much, but at least it gave me something to do. After the final salutes, the graduating class marched off. When they got to the rear of the parade ground, they were finally considered to be finished their training. They were given the final dismissal by the BSM and threw their hats in the air, marking the start of their life as junior officers.

The rest of us marched back to the lines, under the command of our new CSM. Left, right, left, right, left. Halt. The Drilly followed along like an anxious puppy, still snapping at our heels. Our training wasn't over yet, so the Drilly insisted on giving us a debrief on our performance on the parade. Vigilance, always. Never let your standards drop. Etc. We were finally dismissed and waited for the 1st class cadets from our company to return. Whilst we were expected to wait for them to get back so we could congratulate them, I could see that I wasn't the only one who was too cold to stick around. My fingers no longer worked, and I wasn't sure I'd be able to open the door to my room. The only solution was to get some blood back in my fingers and searched around for something that would help warm them up. The bar heater in my room was out of reach so the next best thing was a hot shower. I briefly paused to wonder whether I could get my parade uniform wet, before realizing I was already soaked from the rain. A shower couldn't be any different, I figured and trudged off to the bathroom. My rifle clattered on the floor as I struggled with the taps. Luckily, they offered little resistance and moments later I was standing under a steady torrent of hot water and steam. I clenched and unclenched my hands as my body transferred the warmth of the water into the blood flowing through my veins. As I stood and soaked up the heat, I heard the other showers spark to life and the clatter of rifles on the tiles.

"Fuck, is there anything better than this?" I heard Watts mutter from the cubicle next to me.

"If there is, they can keep it," I replied and we both chuckled.

The bathroom filled up steadily as the rest of the company sought refuge from the cold and tried to get the warmth back into their bones. Our parade boots slipped on the wet floor and we steadied each other as the steel caps on the soles of our boots made little squeals each time they skidded on the tiles. We slapped each other on the back and pointed the newcomers towards empty showers, helping them to remove their rifles along the way. All of the hours we had spent squaring away our parade uniforms no longer mattered. All that mattered right now was getting warm and after that, getting dry. We shared a grin with the cadet next to us, for we shared the same happiness and relief in simply being warm again. At times, the simplicity and hilariousness of it was too much to keep to ourselves as the sounds of muffled laughter filled the air. It took me ten minutes to get back into my room after fiddling with the lock with my wet and slippery hands. I threw my clothes on the ground in a wet pile and dried myself off in front of the heater. Looking at myself in the mirror, I couldn't help but laugh. This 'warrior-in-training' had been reduced to a cold lump of flesh by the parade ground and a bit of Canberra winter. How the hell were we going to lead soldiers deep into the heart of the Mussorian heartland if we couldn't even get into our rooms after graduation parade, I wondered.

With the graduation celebration to be held in the mess that night, the mess bar was out of bounds, so we were planned on making a beeline into town early. I had arranged to meet up with my usual drinking buddies in town but needed a lift to get there. KD and the boys from his company had bludged a lift off one of their classmates. So, after a bit of hustling, Hobbes managed to convince Heather to drop us in town with the very clear message that she would not be picking us up.

"Well, if you won't pick us up, you can at least pay for the drinks," Hobbes said with a grin as jumped out of the car.

She shook her head, gunned the engine and shot off into the traffic. By the time she was out of sight, we had our elbows on the Olim's beer garden bar.

The O-club, as we knew it, was our favorite afternoon drinking spot when we weren't at the mess. The drinks weren't as cheap, but the staff and locals were friendly. They put up with us and we couldn't remember the last time anyone had been thrown out. Rumor had it that the two poker machines in the back bar always paid and the chance to making a few extra bucks rarely got past us, especially those who had been bitten by the gambling bug. I was a mug punter at best, and whenever anyone asked me, I'd offer them the same piece of advice.

"Sure, you could give me $100 and I could take it to the casino and turn it into $0. But, if you give me the same $100 and I took it to the Moose, I guarantee we'll have one a bloody good time."

We whiled away the rest of the afternoon drinking jugs of beer and reminiscing about the last six months. By the time the sun had started to set, we were merrily marching down the road into town, and had already forgotten about the graduating class.

I woke up the next morning with no idea at all what had happened. I checked inside my shoes for my keys and wallet. My clothes were in a pile at the end of the bed and the room had a lingering smell of salty chips and gravy. My head ached and my mouth tasted like licorice, but it looked like I'd made it home in one piece. The licorice taste meant that the ouzo had been out at some stage, which meant it could have only been one person's fault. Walker loved ouzo and it was likely to make an appearance if you got caught up in a shout with him. It was rugged stuff at the best of times, and it smelt even worse the next day. A hot shower and cup of strong instant coffee were first on my to-do list, so I threw myself out of bed and headed towards the showers.

"Jesus, you look terrible," Vinny said when I stumbled into the showers.

"Good. I feel terrible," I muttered in reply.

"What time did you get back last night?" he continued.

"No idea. Late. Very late. Have you seen Watts or Hobbes?" I asked.

"Not yet, but someone mentioned that they heard the big guy bouncing down the corridor when he got home last night," he replied and shook his head.

"Good. At least I know that he'll be in worse shape than me," I replied and blinked my eyes.

With mid-year graduation out of the way, I was desperately looking forward to getting out of the College and spending a bit of time back in 'civvy mode' again. Before we were allowed to leave, all that was left to do was move rooms and then we were be free. My new room was exactly like my old one, only further down the hall. I packed my gear back into the cupboards and drawers, with each item of kit or clothing returning to its familiar position in the new room. Like everything else at the College, our rooms were built to be neat and functional. Comfort was secondary, as besides the inbuilt heater, there was nothing comforting about them. The identical cupboards, drawers, mirrors and desks, were functional in every way. And yet, once they were filled with a new occupant and a scattering of personal items, they felt like home. After the toughest of days of training, we knew that once we got back to our room, we could close the door on the rest of the world. The rest of the College's tough exterior was designed to test our mettle and keep us on our toes, yet our rooms always felt like our safe havens.

As I carted my gear from my old room into my new room, I wondered what new challenges the College was silently plotting for us in the coming months. By now, I knew it was always watching us, testing us, and asking itself, "Are they ready?". I had learned to feel the earth move underneath my feet each time the College shifted its weight and prepare to throw something new at us. After the first six months, I knew I didn't have all the answers yet, but at I knew that I had to be prepared for whatever was next.

With the bulk of my gear in the new room, I was in the process of stuffing the last of my books on the shelves when I heard a knock at the door. I turned around to find my old Platoon Sergeant, now Lieutenant Duncan, standing at the door.

"New room, huh?" she asked from the doorway.

"Yep, you know the drill," I replied stiffly.

"Well, I just wanted to say good luck and..."

"I know. Keep my head down and stop pissing the DS off."

"I was going to say, try to enjoy it. But now you mentioned it, that too," she said and folder her arms.

"Will do. Good luck at your end too and thanks," I replied.

"Thanks? For what?"

"You know, for your help with the charge and not being as much of a dick as the rest of your classmates."

She smiled and shook her head.

"You know this place is a lot easier when you don't try to fight the system. Why don't you give it a go for the next few months and see what happens? If I'm wrong, I'll buy you a drink. What do you reckon?"

I leaned back on my desk to thought about.

"Deal. But if you're wrong, I'm holding you to it... Ma'am," I replied and held out my hand.

She shook my hand and smiled before heading off down the hall.

As the sun started its descent, with our new rooms squared away and rifles handed in, we assembled in front of the company to be given our final dismissal. The new CSM, Heather, smiled at us as she took up a position in front of us.

"Well, we've all made it through another six months and we're another step closer to finally getting out of here. You should all be proud of yourselves for making it this far and I can't wait to work alongside you next term as we make this company the best company in the Corps," she said with a big smile.

Like each new CSM, she was obliged to make the same speech as the CSM before her had made. Each time the hierarchy changed, we went through the same routine and listened to the same speeches. The CSM finished with the usual reminders about looking after ourselves while we were on leave and making sure we came back in one piece. You could almost smell the adrenaline in the air as we were dismissed and headed off for leave.

Back in my room, I unrolled my old swag to see how bad it smelt. Not as bad as I expected, I thought before throwing in an extra blanket and a couple of changes of clothes. I checked to make sure my room was squared away one last time, locked the door and jogged out to the carpark.

"Hurry up, you bloody tourist!" Logan yelled, the motor already running.

I chucked my gear into the back of his old Landcruiser and slammed the back door shut. A couple of swags and an esky was all we needed for a week on the road.

"Get me out of here driver," I said with a smile as he stomped the pedal and we blasted out of the car park in a cloud of smoke. All around us, the rest of the Corps was zipping up their bags, locking their doors and heading for the exits as fast as they could. As we trickled out of the grounds in one's and two's, the College solemnly watched us go and waited for the day we would return again.

The old beast spouted black smoke and the gears whined every time we hit a hill, but we didn't care a bit. The winter sun glittered through the trees as we barreled through the national park towards the coast. First stop, Batemans Bay. We were not detailed planners; our idea was simply to find somewhere to have a beer and then figure it out from there. After months of having every waking moment planned for you, it was good to not have anything specific to do.

"Mate, how good is that first schooner going to taste?" I said as we veered around another blind corner.

"Damn right! Can't wait," he replied with a loose grin.

After an hour of twists and turns along the crumbling bitumen, we finally emerged at the bottom of the range and made a beeline for the front bar of the Bayview. Perched on a bar stool with a cold schooner in hand, we felt like we'd won the lotto. The bar girl smiled at us and asked where we were from.

"Canberra," we replied.

"Where are you headed?"

"Not sure yet. Anywhere we can find a beer and a place to sleep," I said with a smile.

We spent the rest of the week driving down the coast towards Melbourne, sleeping by the beach or in one of the national parks. First priority each day was finding somewhere to burn some bacon and get a pot of coffee on. After that, we'd fill up the esky again and hit the road. We had an old NRMA map in the glovebox that we used as our guide. Our only goal was to keep moving south. As long as we could find Triple J on the radio and a place to sleep each night, we were happy. We laughed our way down the coast, as we told stories about the events of the past six months.

With each day away from the College, we relaxed a little more as we reflected on the adventures we'd had. We started to feel like we'd made it over the hump as we could take the best arse-kicking any of the DS could hand out and still manage to crack a smile. We knew all of the little tricks that cut down the time it took to get our gear squared away for inspections and parades. Our bodies had steadily adapted to the rigors of physical training and we felt stronger than we had at the start of the year. Multi-tasking became a habit, and we could easily clean our rifle and boots, whilst shaving, making a brew and packing up our hootchies. Life had become a series of well-practiced drills, all designed to make us sharper, faster and more efficient in the way we went about our duty. Even when we were on leave, we kept ourselves sharp by going for a run each day, barking out the occasional catchword and unwittingly, keeping in step.

Towards the end of the week, we found ourselves a quiet spot in one of the national parks to set up camp. With no one around, we pulled together a little fire and warmed up a couple of tins of beans on the embers. We burnt some toast and wedged our beers in between the rocks while we ate.

"It's a bit like being on exercise, eh?" Logan said as he poked the fire.

"Kind of," I replied as hot beans spilled off my toast onto the dust.

"How good would it have been to have a fire on that last exercise? My feet were like bloody ice blocks most of the time," he added as the fire crackled to life.

"You bet, but I don't reckon any of the field wing will let that happen anytime soon," I replied.

We shook our heads and pulled on our beers.

"Where do you reckon, you're going to go anyway?" he said after putting his beer back down.

"Dunno, I'm thinking trucks at the moment. I know a bunch of the guys from our company want to go to grunts, but I'm not sure it's my cup of tea. You still thinking of artillery, I suppose?"

"Might as well, don't think anyone else would take me," he replied.

As the sun set the cold night air settled around us and we shuffled closer towards the fire until it made our cheeks red. After our exercises and field training, I had started to feel at home in the bush. I listened for the different animals as they moved around in the scrub and watched the colors die off to leave the blacks and greys of night. I'd never really noticed these things before but after a few weeks in the bush playing soldiers, these things were now a part of life. Lying in our pits each night at stand-to, I'd started to notice the ants as they trudged back to their holes and the colors evaporated out of the vegetation in the disappearing light. Listening for the sounds of my section mates, as they tried to find a comfortable spot amongst the leaves, rocks and tree roots, my eyes were alert for any signs of movement and I tried to remember 'why things are seen' (shape, shine, silhouette, spacing, movement). For a moment, I almost missed not having my rifle and a section of my classmates around me.

"Another beer?" Logan asked, bringing me back to reality.

"Good idea," I replied and reached into the esky.

We'd talk for a while and then listen for a while, content to enjoy nature without any attacks or ambushes to worry about. With the last of the beers emptied and the fire's dying embers glowing softly, we rolled into our swags and were asleep within minutes.

By the end of the week, we were running short of funds and pointed the truck north again. The break had been a good one and although I wouldn't have said no to another week off, I felt like it was time to get back to training. Our adventure had given me an opportunity to have a think about what was next and what I needed to do if I was going to make it to graduation. Even though I still didn't know exactly where I was headed after graduation, at least I now thought I was a decent chance of getting there.

"Home sweet home, eh?" I quipped when we finally turned off the highway towards Canberra.

"Home for now," he replied and punched the accelerator.

Part 3. The Home Stretch

That first Sunday night back in the lines was a shock to the system, and it took a while to get back into routine. We stuffed our civvies back in their hiding spots, ironed the uniforms we had hastily stuffed in our cupboards before we left, gave our boots a polish, and dusted off the shelves. Down the hall I could see our new Platoon Sergeant, Vinny, as he finished moving the last of his stuff into his new room. The new 3rd class would arrive in a week, so for now it was just us and the 2nd class. I had no grudges against the 2nd class in our company, as they seemed a pretty good bunch. I remembered what it had been like when I was in their position and figured we were all in this together.

"Hey mate, welcome back," Vinny called as he dragged one of his trunks down the hall.

"Yeah, good to see you. Need a hand?"

"All good. Did you hear who the new Drilly is?"

"Nah, I was just going to cross my fingers and hope they'd forget to give us one."

We both knew that would never happen.

"It's Ruth," Vinny said with a grin and gave me a thumbs up.

Vinny was a decent rugby player so having Sergeant Ruth as the company Drilly was a win for him.

"Thank fuck for that," I replied.

After my last chat with him, I figured that he'd be less painful than Zimburger had been and so I'd finally get off the shit list. We also had a new OC, Captain Yeoman from tactics wing. So far, I'd managed to stay on his good side, so I crossed my fingers that the next six months would be different to the last.

We had the next week in barracks, brushing up on our platoon defensive tactics and writing military history essays. With our newly issued ranks, we jokingly braced up when one of the CSM's walked past or shouted, "stand fast!" when they walked into the rec room. There was a different feel in the air, and I felt like I could see the light at the end of the tunnel at last. One afternoon as I marched back to the lines, I caught movement out of the corner of my eye.

"Oi! Cadet Rickson get over here," Sergeant Ruth barked as he rounded the corner of the company.

"Yes Sarge," I replied and marched over.

"So, you made it back from leave?" he said, as he tucked his pace stick under his arm.

"Seems that way."

"So, I had a bit of a look through your records this morning...they are not good," he said as he placed his pace stock at his feet and leant on it. I stood silent, wondering whether this was the start of a fresh run on the round-about.

"I also had a look at your grades, and luckily, they are not bad. Not great, but not bad. You might have a chance of making it out of here in six months, but only if you stop fucking around and get on with it."

There was only one answer you could give to his question.

"Yes Sarge, consider it done," I replied, unsure if he'd buy it.

He paused and slowly cracked a smile.

"Good. I hate doing paperwork. So, here's what I want you to do. Every time you get a rush of blood to your head, I want you to pause, zip your trap and play the game. Full stop. You get me?"

"Loud and clear," I replied and snapped myself to attention.

"Righto, let's see you do it then," he said and marched off briskly.

We were due back in the field the next week, which suited me just fine. The less time I had to spend in barracks, the less chance I had to open my mouth and rub someone up the wrong way. The next field exercise would test our ability to practices the defensive tactics we had been taught in our classroom. In the field, we would no longer be able to get away with farming our TEWT stakes, as we would have to dig each of the pits in by hand. This would take us days as we'd have to use the old ET's (entrenching tool) we carried on our packs and would have to be done in between patrols and the expected enemy probes each night.

Checking the section list when it had gone up, I saw I'd landed in a section with few familiar names with one of the crusty Sergeants from the field wing as our DS. Sergeant Baldwin was sharp as a tack and didn't miss a trick in the field. Luckily, I also picked up first swing on the gun, which would give me a few days to get back into field mode before I was due for a run at the Platoon Commanders job. The day before we were due to depart our section organized to meet up out the back of Alamein company to split up stores and have a chinwag about how we would approach the exercise. Trotting down the mess steps after dinner I bumped into one of my section mates as he was heading in the same direction.

"Bensonhurst, how are you old man?"

"Ahhh, Johnny Ricksticks, fancy seeing you here," he said with his usual goofy smile.

We hadn't been in the same section before, even though we often shared a beer at the mess bar. He seemed to share my thoughts on the need to take a more relaxed approach to training and was known for his ability to fall asleep just about anywhere. We ambled down to the back of the company to find the others sitting alongside a pile of section stores. For the next couple of hours, we pulled apart ration packs, distributed the heavy radio batteries, and played paper-scissor-rock for who would carry the remaining stores. I ended up with Logan as number two on the gun, which was fine by me as he had his shit squared away, was never jack with brews and was handy with a joke when things got tough.

"Eh mate, you don't have a jack hammer in your pack do you?" I joked as we pulled apart the ration packs.

"Fuck, I wish. That ground out there is going to be rock hard. If we're lucky, we might get one of the pits that the last class dug out. If we're not..." he replied with a shake of his head.

"Ting, ting, ting," I said and made a digging motion with an invisible pick.

We both grinned and silently hoped that we'd get lucky. The alternative would be digging a new pit and that was guaranteed to suck.

After parade the next morning, we pulled our packs on and marched down to field training wing. The air was still cool and there was a light breeze that reminded us how close we were to the snowy mountains. We gathered around our section DS for roll call and collected our blank ammunition from the Section 2IC. Sergeant Baldwin briefed us on what was expected of us as we sat on our packs waiting for the transport to arrive.

"Righto you lot, on the bus!" yelled one of the DS as the trucks pulled up beside us.

We worked together to pile our packs and assorted stores into the back of the trucks, before hauling ourselves up and waiting for the convoy to depart. Sergeant Baldwin rode in the cab with the driver, leaving us to gossip in the back as we bounced along the highway to the range. The canvas sides were tied down to keep the cold air out and we huddled together amongst our packs on the floor.

"What do you reckon, anyone think we'll see some frost tonight?" I asked from my spot on the floor.

"Hmmm," the Bensonhurst said, finger checking the air, "chances are better than average. As a matter of fact, I'd bet my left nut that it's going to be... dead-set freezing."

The Possum sniffed and blew his nose into his hanky loudly. We knew he hated the cold and that we'd be listening to him sneeze and sniffle every night. The range wasn't far off, and it wasn't long before we felt the trucks lurch and roll as they hit the dirt road at the boundary of the field training area. At this stage we had a pretty good idea which road we were on, but with the sides closed up, we'd be in the dark as to our final destination. The section commander busily studied the map and consulted with the 2IC as the truck bumped down the road. Occasionally, we'd hear the gears grind and the engine would scream as the truck hit another hill.

"Any bets on our starting loc?" Heather asked.

"Tank Hill."

"The 880 feature."

"Parliament house."

"You guys are no help," she said and shook her head.

She was a good hand and was pretty squared-away in barracks but wasn't much chop at field navigation. Luckily, she had Nathan as her 2IC, and he claimed to be pretty handy at all things field related.

"Rest easy lads, I've got this covered. I know this place like the back of my hand," he said, giving us a wink and a grin.

The truck shuddered to a halt and a moment later the back lifted up to reveal the darkly camouflaged face of Sergeant Baldwin.

"Off the bus you lot, you've got sixty seconds to be on the side of the road," he said out of the corner of his mouth.

The tail gate dropped, and we furiously threw our packs, webbing and stores out of the truck. Jumping down onto the hard Majura dirt made our bones rattle. We quickly sifted through the mountain of packs, grabbed our gear and started down the road towards where Sergeant Baldwin was sitting.

"Ok then, where are we now Section Commander?" he asked, pulling a folded map out from his thigh pocket. "And the rest of you lot can get your maps out too. I need an eight-figure grid reference. You've got five minutes."

We pulled our packs into a huddle and got our maps out. Most of the fire trails started to look alike after a while, so you couldn't rely on them to tell you where you were. We looked towards the west, searching for the tent lines at the main camp and beyond to Mount Majura. Even on a cloudy day like today, it towered over the horizon with its spindly radio towers confirming where the high point was. Looking south, we could see glimpses of the airport, but couldn't make out any of the other landmarks. We sought out the other high points that we knew, took bearings with our compasses and estimated distances before drawing a web of lines on our maps. Looking around at the group, some were still attempting to find hills to use, others were scratching their heads at the vague collection of lines on their map and a few were still trying to orient their map to the ground.

"Times up! Righto, where are we section commander?" Sergeant Baldwin said and walked over to where Heather was sitting.

Heather stood up and pointed to her map.

"I'm pretty sure we are just about... here," she said, not looking confident.

Baldwin studied her map and the marks she had drawn on it. "Are you sure, section commander?"

Heather looked at the map again, trying to align it to her bearings.

"Yes, I think so," she offered.

"Give me a grid reference then," he replied.

Heather sat down, laid her map across her knee and pulled a protractor out of her field notebook. She moved the transparent plastic tool over the map, squinting to read the increments.

"Ahhh, 0288..9697?" she replied

"Anyone else think that is right?" he asked and looked around.

We looked at our maps.

"Anyone game enough to use that grid reference to call in fire support from?"

We looked sheepishly at our maps and shook our heads.

"You've got two minutes to confirm where in the hell we are. I hope we are just shaking out the cobwebs here people. Otherwise, this is going to be a long week."

Our section navigation guru sat next to Heather and they re-did the resection again while the rest of us checked our calculations and looked for features to help us orientate ourselves. After another go at it, Sergeant Baldwin was happy with the answer and he gave us our first check point to patrol to. We were glad to be underway and slung our heavy packs onto our backs before shaking out into patrol formation. From here on in, we were back in field mode. The first day or so of silence was always strange, as you slowly became accustomed to being without the day-to-day noise and chatter that surrounded us in barracks. Besides the rustling of the bushes beneath our feet and the occasional plane overhead, there were no sounds other than those provided by the bush around us. We could hear kangaroos as they thumped by in the scrub and the occasional call of a bird in the trees. In some ways, it was actually pretty relaxing, and there were times when I enjoyed the steady trudge of patrolling. Sure, my pack seemed to find new ways of digging into your shoulders and sweat dripped into my eyes through the cam cream, but it beat having a Drilly chew you out for the state of your boots or the PTI's making you run the scramble track. As we crested a small rise, we heard the first sounds of an attack taking place in the distance. The radio crackled to life as we heard one of the call signs report in.

"Zero-alpha, this is two-two-bravo. Contact, over."

This initial call alerted the other patrols to keep the channel clear and prepare to assist. Heather looked at Sergeant Baldwin, who nodded. She put an arm up in the air, motioning for us to halt. We all passed the signal along, checking to make sure the person behind us had seen it and then finding a place to drop to the ground. Logan drew up to me and plonked down beside me. Looking around, I saw the rest of the section doing the same. Except the Bensonhurst who had missed the sign and was still bobbing along at the end of the rifle group, eyes firmly fixed on the ground in front of him. Sergeant Baldwin heard him coming and tossed a rock in his direction. It ricocheted off a tree in front of him and he froze, looking around to see where it had come from. Realizing that he was the only one still on his feet, he dropped to the ground. Logan and I shook our heads, quietly chuckling to ourselves. Heather and the 2IC listened to the radio trying to figure out what we'd do next. Depending on how far off we were, we'd either harbor up here and wait until the shooting was done or continue on our way. After a minute Nathan looked up and gave us the harbor signal followed by the signal for 'grab a smoke and a brew'. We knew we'd be here for at least ten minutes, so we dropped our packs and made ourselves comfortable on the ground. I pulled down the bipod legs on the gun and looked around for a spot with as few rocks as possible.

"Brew?" Logan whispered.

"Does the pope shit in the woods?" I replied as I heard him retrieve his cooking gear.

It had been drilled into us during field training, that we should always make the most of every spare minute we had in the field. There was rarely a moment that didn't require you to be doing something, whether it be cleaning your rifle, setting up your hootchie or running perimeter cord. Ten minutes in the field was the equivalent of thirty minutes in barracks and was more than enough time to throw together a brew. In less than two minutes, a cup of coffee sat steaming in cups canteen. He touched it up with sweetened condensed milk and offered me a swig, all the while puffing on a cigarette he'd produced from his pack. As we heard the shots start to die down, the 2IC came around to each of us and whispered, "Leaving in two minutes, pack your shit up."

Minutes later, as promised, we were on our feet again, humping towards what we hoped would be our final destination for the day. Somehow, we managed to avoid the enemy for the rest of the afternoon and as the sun began to descend towards the western horizon, we pulled up just short of a large sparsely covered hill. We propped down on our knees and faced out to wait for our orders. We knew at some stage we were going to meet up with the rest of the platoon to site our defensive position and hoped this would be it. The 2IC came around and gave us a quick heads up as we waited.

"This is the spot lads," he said quietly and pointed to the hill in front of us, "We're just waiting on the word from PHQ, then we'll do the recce."

"Tops. Let's hope you can find us somewhere soft," I replied.

"Even better, find us a spot with a bar and a waterbed," added Logan.

"You've got Buckley's," he said and grinned, "I'm sure Baldwin has found an ants nest for you two blokes already."

Logan and I gave him the finger as he departed, hoping he was joking.

The next half an hour was spent patrolling around and over the hill, before setting up a temporary harbor to wait for the other sections. Eventually, we saw movement at the bottom of the hill and waited for the other sections to approach. The scouts bumbled up the hill in our direction and grinned when they saw us. The sweat had started to smudge their cam cream and their faces looked like they'd been rubbed in ash. We went through the challenge procedure and they marched up into our position past our gun. Whispered hello's and grins were exchanged as they walked past us and into the center of the position. An hour or so later and we repeated the process again as the next section arrived. Across the other side of the hill, we could hear the other platoons repeating the routine as they occupied their positions on the hill. In all we'd have a company's worth of cadets spread across the position, which was to be our last line of defense against the Mussorian hordes that were once again headed in our direction.

We waited for Dig, the Platoon Commander, to come around to check, then double check our positions before deciding on exactly where we'd end up. As he walked around the hill, we exchanged a few words and tried to get him to find us a spot where the ground was soft. Try as we might, each pit was double-checked by the DS to make sure it aligned with the company position. I looked at Logan beside me when they'd left and shrugged my shoulders.

"A lovely view, not many rocks and the smell of eucalyptus. What more could we ask for?" I whispered.

"Someone else to dig the pit for us," he replied with a sly grin.

This would now be our home for the next week as we'd have to dig ourselves in to defend the hill against the mighty Mussorian brigade that was theoretically heading our way. Looking around at the rest of the sections, we didn't seem to have done do badly. Our pit was beside an old dead tree on top of what looked like it might have been one of the positions from the previous year. The ground was still fairly uneven and there was the odd rock or two sticking out from the surface, possibly from a previous owner who had been a bit hasty when he filled the pit in. We hoped that it would be mostly loose earth and the odd rock once we got beneath the surface, but chances were there might be a few surprises in there too. Either way, we got what we got, so it wasn't worth complaining any more about it.

With the sun almost on the horizon, we knew wouldn't be digging tonight, so we settled into our evening routine and waited for stand-to to be called. After the clearing patrols came back in, we hoisted up our hootchies and crawled into our sleeping bags in the hope of a night of unbroken sleep. Those lucky enough to get an early shift had the best chance of a decent night's sleep, but that depended on the plans of the DS. Fortunately, there was only one probe that night, which we all thought was very decent of the DS for a change. We knew it would get worse after we started to dig and dived straight back into our still warm sleeping bags once stand-down was given.

After morning routine, the next day, we started to dig in earnest. The guns remained manned, but only with one person at a time. We started by marking out the orientation and length of our pits, checking them with the DS to make sure they were the regulation size. When they were finished, they needed to be deep enough for us to stand up in, so we had our work cut out for us. They would also have sleeping bays dug into them, to protect us from any surprise mortar rounds that might find us while we slept. Even though we only had our issued ET's to dig with, we made good progress through the day as we cleared the loose top layer from the old pit. Our 2IC eventually scavenged a few full-sized shovels for us from the company stores, which made things move a bit quicker. Digging with the Army issued ET might have been possible, but it was far from efficient. Somewhere else on the position, we heard the sounds of motorized diggers and pestered the 2IC anytime we saw him to get them sent down to us.

Once a day, we'd be required to form part of a clearing patrol and would hand-over our positions to teams from the other platoons before heading out. At least these patrols didn't require us to carry our packs, so they were a welcome relief from the digging. Inevitably, we'd run into the enemy someone on the route and would have to fight our way across the rocky terrain to kill or capture a couple of the Mussorians who had snuck up on us. Over time, we were quickly able to recognize their foreign jungle fatigues and the different weapons they carried. The noise of their carbines was different from our own rifles and before long, we could instantly hear the loose metal on metal sound they made after each shot.

Around mid-afternoon, we defeated a small patrol of Mussorians on a rise about a kilometer from our position and gathered in for the debrief. Sergeant Baldwin ran us through the battle as he'd seen it before handing over to the enemy to describe what they saw. He was not one to mince words and identified anyone whose fire and movement skills were not up to his expectations. The section commander was given a chance to explain her side of the story and we all tried our best to help out any time we were asked. There was an unwritten rule that you didn't jack on the section commander, no matter what you thought of them in barracks. If they pointed you at a position you knew was going to result in a kick in the backside, you modified it accordingly and when asked, told the DS that was what you thought the section commander had intended. As the debrief ended we sat up and pulled our webbing back on.

"Before you lot shoot off, do you mind if I have a word?"

We looked around behind us to see the RSM in full battle gear, his face heavily camouflaged and his pack bulging up over his shoulders. Sergeant Baldwin nodded and moved out of his way as he joined him in front of us.

"Enemy platoon, good job. You can go now," he said and grabbed a seat on a tree stump.

He took a deep breath in and looked around at the section for a minute.

"Thank you, Sergeant Baldwin. Now, as you lot may know, I had the pleasure of spending a bit of time on a couple of government sponsored trips to Vietnam in the 70's. And while I was there, I learned a few lessons I think might be helpful."

Our ears were still ringing from our skirmish, so we shuffled ourselves into a tight huddle. There wasn't a cadet in the Corps who didn't respect the RSM. He was a professional soldier in every way, tough, disciplined and a master of his trade. When he spoke, we listened.

"So, there was this one day when we'd just finished clearing our way through an area that the yanks had bombed with their B-52's. There were massive craters everywhere and we decided to use one as a harbor while we pulled up for lunch. At the time I was a young and eager, just like you lot. I sat back on my pack, pulled my webbing off and had all of my crap spread out around me. Next minute, I look over to the bloke on the gun and see him giving me the enemy signal," he said and held one arm out with the thumb pointing down.

"I looked across at him and said, 'Mate, it's just the clearing patrol, don't worry about it,' to which he replied, 'Yeah, well when was the last time you saw one of our clearing patrols wearing black pajama's!' Well, I legged it over to him and we hooked in for the next couple of hours," he paused and looked around to make sure we were all listening.

"In the end, we cleared the place back up again, but with no help from me as I didn't have my webbing on and had run out of ammo halfway through the kick-on. Now, have a look around. How many of you have pouches undone, rifles more than an arm's length away and stuff spread all over the place? One day you very well may end up on the two-way range and when you do, you will need to be squared away if you are going to be able to do your job."

There was no menace in his voice, but the message was loud and clear. He pulled himself to his feet and hoisted his pack on his back. As he did, we silently checked our gear, our fingers closing open pouches, pulling loose webbing straps and feeling for our weapons. On the way back to the position, he humped along beside Heather and Sergeant Baldwin, quietly discussing how she could improve next time.

"Ahh, home sweet home," I said as we arrived back at our pit.

"And look what they've done to the place since we've been away," Logan said and started pulling out his brew gear.

It started to rain that night and it didn't take long before we were soaked to the bone. The first times it rained on exercise, all I could think about was getting under a hootchie and into some dry gear again. But it didn't take long before you got used to being wet and understand the wisdom of our field staff who repeatedly reminded us, "If it ain't raining, it ain't training."

Still, it didn't stop us from cursing the skies each time they turned grey and crossing our fingers in the hope that the rain would leave us alone. We knew that as long as we keep ourselves warm, being wet wasn't the worst thing that could happen. When you're wet, the only luxury you have left is the possibility of getting your boots off at night and, hopefully get a dry pair of socks on the next day. This was tough when you were standing in a waist deep pit that was filling with winter rain, but we reminded ourselves of the hell that the ANZACs had been through and how lucky we were instead.

That night the probe was early, and the enemy decided to cleared out after setting off a couple of trip flares on the eastern perimeter. Even better, our section 2IC had managed to roster our two Fijian on picket together around midnight. They were not known for their ability to stay awake and predictably fell asleep. We slept soundly only to be roused by Sergeant Baldwin when he found them on his pre-dawn inspection of the perimeter. Our wake-up call that morning was the sound of Baldwin giving them a decent arse-chewing.

"Getupyoulazyfucks! What the fuck do you think you're fucking doing!" he barked and gave them both a nudge with his boot.

Bleary eyed and totally confused, they sat bolt upright. The rest of us quickly scooted out of our farters and dropped our hootchies, whilst pulling our boots and webbing on at the same time. As we bunkered down in our pits, we looked across at the others and chuckled quietly, glad it wasn't us.

After morning routine, we rotated positions again and I bid the now waist deep pit I'd shared with Logan goodbye and headed off around the perimeter. As luck had it, I lobbed in beside Bensonhurst, who had scored some soft ground and was almost at chest depth.

"Welcome to The Hotel Bensonhurst," he said as I chucked my gear in beside him.

"Tidy work mate, this place looks like the Hilton compared to my old pit," I said.

"Yes, the chandelier is due to be delivered today and as you can see, the pool is almost finished," he replied and gestured towards the bush in front of the pit.

I jumped down into the pit beside him to survey his handiwork. The edges of the pit were rough but almost square and it was almost at regulation depth. At one end, he'd dug in a ledge that housed his gas burner and an assortment of brew gear. He followed my gaze and reached down to grab the cups-canteen that sat atop the stove.

"Café a la Bensonhurst," he said and offered the mug to me.

"Don't mind if I do, thanks mate," I replied.

We shared the remnants of sticky ration pack coffee as we got back into the routine of digging. As the hours passed, we edged deeper and deeper into the red dirt. The spoil formed a little mound in front of the pit, which at some stage we'd have to use to fill sandbags. Across the hill, the sounds of industrious cadets could be heard through the trees as they slowly, but surely tunnelled into the earth.

The rest of the week followed the same pattern, as the enemy continued their offensive. Patrol by day, get probed by night. As each day passed, you felt your field skills sharpening and could see your section mates around you slip into their routines. Sergeant Baldwin loosened up a bit, but never missed a beat. His acid tongue managed to leave its mark at least once a day and he never let anyone off who didn't pull their weight during an attack. Our pits got deeper and a few even reached the full depth, so the DS had them start digging sleeping bays. The cam cream dug deeper into our pores and our bush razors got blunter by the day. We 'bombed up' on ammo and water each morning and did clearing patrols each afternoon. Even though we were separated by generations from our ancestors who had gone before us, we started to get the feel of what it meant to be soldiers.

With the week drawing to a close, most of the pits were deep enough to stand in and we knew the final assault couldn't be far off. I'd finally rotated through all of the positions and found myself in the section commander's spot as we headed up for nighttime orders. I had Bensonhurst as my 2IC and the two of us wandered up the hill together towards the Platoon Commander's pit.

"Besides being cold, wet and miserable, I'm giving this hotel a three-star rating," Bensonhurst said on the way up with his usual optimism.

"Plus, I think the section has killed at eight, maybe nine Mussorians. Chalk one up to the good guys," I replied with a thumbs up.

We figured we'd be getting close to the end of the exercise, with the likelihood that we wouldn't be getting much sleep that night. At the orders group, the platoon commander ran us through our night orders and the designated actions that we would take once the Mussorians reached us. By now we knew the drill well enough and asked questions that we hoped would make him sound like he knew what he was doing, even though we knew the answers already. The result would be the same either way. We'd be probed all night and then around dawn, have the lot thrown at us from all sides. After that, our most likely next step was to abandon the hill and pull out. The plan was to pack up and march out via the back end of the hill under the cover of notional artillery fire. If we were in luck, the DS might have organized some engineer support to put some 'bang' in the ground that they would detonate as we got off the hill to make it feel like the real thing. Even though we knew they weren't real, the sound of explosives was almost certain to get the heart racing and the feet moving a bit faster. Back at the position we briefed our pits and checked everyone had enough ammo before hunkering down for stand-to.

We toyed with putting our two sleepers on picket together again, as we figured we weren't going to get much sleep anyway but decided against it as it would tempt getting a kick in the backside by Sergeant Baldwin if he found out. Bensonhurst and I put ourselves on last swing, as we figured we'd be awake by then either way.

"Mate, how good is the mog ride home going to be tomorrow?" Bensonhurst said as we finished our inspection of the pits.

"You'll be asleep by the time we hit the gate," I replied.

We clinked our brew mugs, tossed the remnants into the bushes and headed off to put our hootchies back up for the night.

As predicted, we didn't have to wait long until the first probe that night. I'd just hit the initial stages of deep sleep when I heard the first shots from one of the enemy carbines ring out in the still night air. I kicked the Possum beside me, who was the section radioman and was sharing the hootchie. I'd left my boots on as I knew what was in store, so all I had to do was grab my webbing and rifle before jumping into our pit.

"Poss," I hissed in the dark.

I could hear him rustling about behind me, obviously caught up in his sleeping bag.

"Fuck Poss, get moving mate, we need comms."

Another couple of shots rang out and then the first flare went up as the first wave of enemy managed to find one of our trip wires.

Possum climbed in beside me, huffing and puffing.

"Are you alright mate?" I asked.

"Yeah, couldn't find the zipper on my bloody bivvy bag. Almost had to cut my way out," was his whispered reply.

"Happens mate. Now get the comms up," I whispered back. I looked around for any sign of Sergeant Baldwin. If he was here, then I'd expect we were in it for the long haul. If not, he was probably saving himself for later. We stood-to in our pits and waited. Ten minutes, nothing. Fifteen minutes, nothing. Eventually the radio crackled to life and told us to stand-down. I shuffled around the position and stood everyone down.

"Looks like there will be no beauty sleep for us tonight," Logan said as I gave him the good news.

"Won't do you any good anyway," I said in reply.

"Speak for yourself, there are plenty of ladies out there who considered me to be ruggedly handsome," he fired back.

I followed the perimeter cord back to the hootchie and tucked myself back into my farter again, even though I didn't hold much hope that I'd be there for long.

Sure enough, the enemy turned up again an hour later, this time with a bit more effort. They threw some whizz-bangs and fired off a bunch of rounds out front of our section. We scurried back to our pits and tried to make out their positions in the blackness. Even in the sparse scrub, without a flare to provide some light we couldn't make out a thing. Our orders were to hold our fire unless we knew exactly where the enemy was and even then, the guns were to stay silent so as not to give away their position.

"Pricks," I said as I leaned against my rifle, trying to keep my eyes open.

"At least it's not raining," said Poss and we both chuckled

I wasn't sure whether he had been trying to make a joke or whether we were that tired that we laughed anyway. We strained our eyes trying to pick up some movement and flinched each time a twig snapped in the darkness. The blank rounds we used on exercise were pretty loud and after firing hundreds of them during our mock battles during the week, most of us had a permanent ringing in the ears that made listening in the dead of night pretty much impossible. But we tried; after all, we were cadets and that was what we did.

The rest of the night continued in the same fashion. At one stage I wasn't sure whether I'd gone to bed at all. As I stood in my pit with my cheek pressed against my rifle, all I could think about was a warm bed and for some reason, a cup of hot soup. Sergeant Baldwin brought me back to reality by sitting on the edge of our pit and asking, "What's the story section commander?"

I turned around and it took me a moment to realize who he was. I'm sure he saw how dazed I was but didn't mention it.

"Ahh, enemy out front Sarge. We think there might be two of them, but we haven't seen any movement in a while," I blurted out.

"Have you reported it to the platoon commander?" he asked.

I paused, my mind still fuzzy. Searching through the scrambled kaleidoscope of my recent memory I found nothing.

"I think so," was the best I could do.

"Well best you make sure there young Rickson. Wouldn't want the platoon commander keeping everyone awake all night because of you."

Shit! I hadn't told the Platoon Commander, so everyone was waiting on me.

"Poss, get on the blower to PHQ and let 'em know we've had a couple out front of us, but they look like they've left," I said.

Possum got on the radio and relayed my message. I could hear the platoon commander on the other end and knew his response wasn't pleasant.

"He said…" started Possum.

"Yeah, I heard it," I replied.

We waited another ten minutes and then called back in to report that we had no more movement. After what seemed like hours later, we got the stand-down again.

As we'd guessed, the final probes started when I was on picket with Bensonhurst just before the first rays of dawn crept over the horizon. By then we'd managed to grab a couple of broken hours shut eye, which guaranteed everyone would be pretty slow off the mark when things kicked off. The first thing we heard were a few whizz-bangs going off in front of the section to our right.

"Piss off," I said, barely opening my eyes.

Bensonhurst was asleep, slumped against the end of the pit.

"Bensonhurst, wake up," I said and gave him a kick.

"What, huh, who…" he stammered and shook his head.

As tired as we were, his movements looked comical and I had to laugh.

"The 101 Mussorian Regiment are finally here mate, time to shake a leg," I laughed.

"Do you think we've got time for a brew?" he yawned.

"Of course, but you're making it," I replied, hoping he was serious.

Around us we could hear the sound of cadets jumping into trenches as the hill came alive. Bensonhurst dragged himself up to a stand. "Right, what do you want me to do then boss?" he asked.

Then it came to me, I was the section commander, not the gunner. "Go check the other pits and make sure they're all up. Let 'em know to start packing their gear up if they can," I said.

"On it boss," he said and shot off with one hand on the perimeter cord.

Moments later, the gunner and his number two jumped into the pit beside me.

"Righto, I'm up. What's next?" Logan said as he handed me my rifle.

"Same as usual," I replied, letting him take his place back on the gun.

"Yep, I know the one. Hurry up and wait," he nodded with a weary grin.

I crawled out of the pit and reached for the perimeter cord that led back to my pit. Sergeant Baldwin was there with Possum when I got back.

"What's going on section commander?" he asked.

"I think the blokes next door have been bumped," I replied. "Poss, have you checked-in with PHQ?"

"Sure have. They think the enemy are mustering out in front of two platoon."

"Anything else?"

"Nothing at this stage."

Good, I thought. Not that I didn't like my classmates from two platoon, as I knew we'd all get our chance. I was just glad it was them for now.

"Ahh, anything else I need to do Sarge?" I said, looking up to Sergeant Baldwin.

"I don't know section commander, what do you think?" he replied and looked at me through squinted eyes.

That was about the worst answer he could give, as it didn't tell me I was doing anything wrong. Or right. Bensonhurst came hustling up the path and crouched down besides us.

"G'day Sarge, nice morning for it," he offered with a grin that I could only just make out in the pre-dawn light.

"Yeah, what's so good about it," he sneered.

"Ahh you know, the enemy have finally made it here and we're all up. Sounds like a party, don't you reckon?" Bensonhurst said.

I thought he was delirious, and the scene started to seem a little surreal. On one side we heard the sounds of a battle raging and yet where we were, only a hundred odd meters away, we were having a quiet chat about how nice the morning was. If this was war, then sign me up, I thought.

Sergeant Baldwin reminded me to do another round of the perimeter to check on the rest of the section and make sure they squared their gear away. I shook off the tiredness and rushed around the pits, as the shooting match continued in front of two platoon.

By the time I was back in my pit, the siege had spread across our frontage. In the early morning light, the thump of 'wombat guns' (grenade launchers) could be heard from various spots around the position as they fired flares to illuminate the approaching enemy. Unlike the earlier probes, we could now identify the enemy positions and were given the orders to return fire. With the dawn approaching we could hear the heavy machine guns in the middle of the position let rip as they joined the attack now that the enemy were close. When the battle ebbed, we hurriedly stuffed our gear back in our packs and checked our pits for any loose equipment. I cursed the timing of it all, as that brew that Bensonhurst had mentioned would have put a bit of extra fuel in the tank. Instead, we chewed on cold muesli bars and threw back the cold contents of our water bottles. Sergeant Baldwin walked around the pits, checking that we were playing by the rules and not just shooting for the sake of it. I remember at one stage looking over at Bensonhurst to see him alternating between his rifle and a set of finger pistols. I almost fell over laughing when he saw me and blew the smoke off the top of one of them. Lucky Sergeant Baldwin didn't see him, as he would have definitely failed to see the humor in it.

With the sun now well over the horizon, we got the order to retreat, or advance in a rearward direction as some of DS put it. I got Bensonhurst to pass the order around to shoulder packs and get ready for the word. Possum did a fine job of pulling our hootchie down but couldn't shove everything into his pack as he also had the radio. We dragged the loose gear into the pit and in between taking turns shooting at the enemy, we managed to get our packs closed with our gear loosely shoved into them.

I remember loading my last full magazine when the radio cackled to life, and we received the order to bug out. I signaled to the other pits and we lifted up to start the march back to where we were told the trucks would be waiting.

"You alright with that radio, Poss?" I asked as we humped our badly loaded packs up the incline.

"Yeah, I'm good," he replied, his back bent.

I checked we had everyone as we neared the crest of the hill. Bensonhurst was at the rear and gave me a double thumbs up as he reached me.

"Fuck, I almost had those blokes," he said, "another few more minutes and we would have won that."

We high fived and I jumped in behind him. You had to hand it to him, he knew how to keep smiling at the worst of times. Heading down the hill in single file we bee-lined along the dirt road towards our pick-up point. At the bottom of the hill, we could see a line of trucks parked in a clearing and we humped along with a smile on our faces.

An hour later as our feet thumped along the dirt roads south towards Canberra, we realized why our DS had been smiling during the retreat. They knew there was more fun in store and Sergeant Baldwin' wry grin was definitely a bit bigger than usual when he gave us the 'good news' at the end-ex area.

"Ok Sarge, which Mog's ours?" I asked as we pulled up on the flat.

"You want the good news or bad news first?" he replied.

"Might as well make it the bad news, I guess," I said with a wince.

"Bad news is that we lost the battle and the Mussorians over-ran our position," he said sternly.

"And the good news?" I asked.

"The good news is that the roads back to the College are all out of their artillery range. So, we can walk back safely."

Fuck off, I wanted to say, and I could tell my face must have partially said it. He grinned back at me.

"Best you go tell the rest of the section," he said and looked at his watch.

"Tell 'em they have twenty minutes to re-pack their gear and do their morning routine. We're second in line after PHQ. And lucky for you, you get to be section commander all the way home too."

"Seen. I'll tell 'em now," I said, knowing they'd be just as deflated to hear this as I was.

We were all well and truly rooted from the lack of sleep the night before and had hung our hats on an easy ride home. I took a deep breath and walked over to where the section was sitting on their packs.

"Who wants the good news first?" I asked.

"Pick me, pick me," Hobbes replied with his usual grin.

"We're walking home," I said, and everyone looked up at me.

"You're fucking kidding," said Heather and put her head in her hands.

"Nope, single file, behind PHQ on the road in twenty minutes. It sucks, but it's what we've got," I said and shrugged my shoulders, before adding, "Just think about how good that hot shower is going to be when we're done."

We cursed and moaned but got on with it as we knew a march back without our gear sorted would be a nightmare. At least there wouldn't be any need to worry about the enemy on the way, so we re-balanced our packs by placing all of the heavy stuff at the bottom and dumped what rubbish we could. We shared brews and munched on the limited rations we had left. With a couple of minutes left, the PHQ runner came around and let us know we were moving, so we lined up on the road in a loose single file.

The first couple of kilometers seemed to take forever as we stumbled one foot in front of the other along the red dirt tracks. Every now and then, you'd see someone shrug their pack up a bit higher or wrestle with their webbing around to stop it from pinching. We sipped on the stale water in our water bottles whilst passing around any ration pack chocolate that was left. Sergeant Baldwin marched at the back of the section in the steady rhythm of a professional soldier. A couple of hours later, with grey clouds overhead and the cold winter wind in our faces, we reached the College gates. In our heads, we counted down the steps ahead of us and dreamed of hot showers. We knew we still had a few hours of administration to go when we got in, but that was a welcome change to humping our packs. As we approached the armoury, Sergeant Baldwin pointed towards a tree and we peeled off quietly, happy to have reached our destination.

"Righto, section commander, there's our spot. You know the deal, get 'em going," he said and kept marching towards where the rest of the DS were standing.

We spent the remaining hours cleaning the guns, accounting for our stores and doing the multiple inspections needed for them to be accepted by the armoury staff. At the same time, the DS pulled each of us aside to debrief us on our performance. Sergeant Baldwin's approach to debrief was the same as his approach for everything else and was the verbal equivalent of 'up the guts with plenty of smoke'. He didn't mince words and wasted no time getting to the point. I was left with no illusions that I still had plenty to learn, but he was satisfied that I'd done enough to pass. After the stores were all handed in and the last debrief complete, we were given the nod by the field training team that we were done. The relief was visible across the sea of dirty faces as we slowly marched back to our lines for a hot shower and a fresh set of clothes.

There were still a few hours left in the day so I figured I'd get ahead on the inevitable cleaning that would be needed to get my gear into inspection shape for Monday morning. Along with a handful of others, I begrudgingly dragged my filthy stuff out to the back of the company with a cold coke in the other hand. We hung our packs up on the walls so they could be blasted with the hose before being scrubbed along with our muddy ETs and boots. Sleeping bags were turned inside out to reveal the remnants of ration packs, leaves, sticks and the occasional bush critter that had hitched a lift. Fits of laughter burst out from time to time, as each of us told stories about the antics that our sections had gotten up to. Looking across the courtyard, I saw Heather shaking her head at her filthy pack.

"Are you having fun yet?" I asked.

She dropped her pack and shrugged.

"When does this shit ever stop?"

"In December. Maybe," I replied and we both grinned.

Looking across at the others as they washed, scrubbed and laughed, I thought these moments made the rest of it all worthwhile.

After a solid weekend of celebrating and getting as much sleep as I could, I was feeling good Sunday afternoon. BC Day inspections were a bit more relaxed now we were in 1st class. The weeks ahead would be no doddle though, as we were getting closer to the 'pointy end' of the season. Besides the field modules, we had plenty of other key tests to get through before we were deemed worthy of graduating. Of these, the final tactics assessment was the one that made most of us nervous. But it was a good nervousness, and it was mixed with a splash of adrenalin as we knew we were one step closer to the finish line. We finally allowed ourselves to think that the light we saw at the end of the tunnel wasn't just another train and maybe, just maybe, we would make it through to graduation.

The rest of the week passed without much fuss. More PT, lessons and the usual morning parades. Our primary concern for the week was making it through to the dining-in on Friday night. This would be the final formal dining-in night for us for the year and we could feel the energy build as the week progressed. We spent the nights checking our mess kits, as it was a formal event attended by the DS, our uniforms were expected to be at the same standard as any other parade uniform.

"Ok everyone," the CSM said to the company after the Friday morning parade, "I expect nothing but your best behavior tonight. Anyone who mucks up at the dinner will be in the OC's office first thing Monday morning. You are representatives of the company and are expected to behave like it."

She finished by looking directly at me. I smiled and held my hands up as if to say, "Who me?". I knew the best intentions were no match for a room full of boisterous young cadets and free drinks.

A few of us had arranged to meet up in Hobbes's room before the festivities started. This was partially to do a lastminute check on our gear but also, to sneak in a pre-dinner drink. Even though an early evening portos tempted trouble, the Corps was buzzing with activity before a dining-in, so it was unlikely anyone would be checking. I bounded up the hall to Hobbes's room, found his door was unlocked and pushed my way in to find they'd already started. Watts was sitting on his desk and handed me a beer.

"Beer, one by, for your disposal," he quipped.

"Giddy-up," I replied and twisted the cap off.

"Here's cheers lads," he said and raised his beer, "let's get amongst it!"

"Here's to drinking on the PMC's tab," I added, and we cheered again.

When the beers were all empty, we joined the rest the rest of our classmates as they climbed the stairs to the mess. Looking around, I could see we weren't the only ones who had got an early start on the evening as we merrily made our way inside. First priority was to find out which tables we were sitting on. If we were lucky, we would draw seats a long way from the head table without any senior officers around us. Worst case, we'd end up on the head table, sitting next to one of the cadet hierarchy or one of the senior staff. None of us had drawn hosting duty, which left us to our own devices for the evening. The next step was to swoop the sherry table and do as much damage as we could before the mess bell rang. Like most cadets, I had no idea what sherry was or what service it performed, other than as a drinkable ornament at the start of dining-ins. The mess staff used shot glasses of dry and sweet sherry to make the letters R-M-C on a big table outside the dining room. Most cadets despised the stuff and chose to head to the bar for something more civilized. But not us. Finishing off the sherry table was an old tradition and also an opportunity for a few more free drinks.

"Righto, lads. Where do we start?" I asked the others who were game enough.

"Let's start with the C," said Watts.

"Any more takers? C it is then. Ready... begin!" I said and we grabbed for one of the glasses that made up the C.

Sweet sherry is exactly that, sweet. Sort of like a cross between cheap port and blackcurrant cordial, but with smell of alcohol. We grimaced as we threw down the first shot, before going back for a second. A couple of minutes later and the C was no longer there. We high-fived each other and grinned at how hilarious we thought we were. A couple of 3rd class joined us, and we were halfway through the M by the time the mess bell rang, warning us we had five minutes to be seated. The bell was also a warning that we had best sneak in a final visit to the bathroom, as we wouldn't be able to leave the table until the dinner was finished.

"Corps!" the PMC barked from his place, and we braced up for the CO as he entered the room.

I was seated at the end of one of the 'legs' of the table, mixed up between a couple of my classmates and a couple of 3rd class cadets I didn't know. One of the tactics DS, Captain Schwartz was at the end of the table with the Long Tan CSM. That was good, as we knew she'd do a good job of keeping him occupied discussing Army related topics and making small talk. This left the rest of us to ourselves, which suited me fine.

The first bit of the night was pretty standard fare. We belted down the entrée and mains, and slowly but steadily drank our way through the carafes of wine that circled the table. Olly was next to me and the two of us made sure the wine stayed within arm's reach, guaranteeing ourselves the chance of a quick refill if anyone asked us to pass it their way. At the end of the table, we could see Heather slowly getting into the spirit of the evening, as she didn't mind a drink but was always worried about any staff that might see her enjoying herself too much. The RAAFie bloke beside Heather looked like he had just turned fifteen and sipped his wine like it was hot tea in the middle of summer. We prodded him to have a proper go, but he wasn't having any of it. He was too concerned with putting on a good show and spent most of the night listening intently to Captain Schwartz.

"How'd you go on the ex?" I asked Olly as I filled my glass for the umpteenth time.

"Which bit?" he replied from the seat beside me.

"All of it," I said and passed the carafe.

"Well, the first bit was all right. The middle bit sucked and the last bit really sucked!" he quipped and filled his glass again.

Dessert turned up next and we dutifully polished it off with as much wine as we could. The speeches seemed to drag on for hours, but eventually, the port decanters were set at the end of each table and we knew the end was close.

"To the Queen," the PMC said loudly.

We all stood from our chairs and raised our glasses.

"To the Queen," we echoed and drank.

Some sipped and grimaced, as the mess port was an acquired taste. The rest of us tossed back the whole thing and slammed our glasses back on the table. Taste be stuffed, we weren't here to admire the stuff, we were here to have a good time! The decanters were passed down the line and we all refilled our glasses again. The height of a good pour was the achievement of glass that was filled to the brim, with the occasional spillage resulting. We jibbed and laughed at each other as each cadet down the table tried to ensure their glasses were filled to the brim. By now, all but the staunchest of DS had relaxed and we no longer worried too much about who was around us.

"To the Army," said the CSM and we followed suite.

I could feel my teeth floating after the second toast and wondered whether all of those sherry's were a good idea. My vision blurred for a second before I heard Olly whisper, "Dude, you alright?"

"Never better," I said and shook my head.

The blurriness subsided and I tried to focus on Heather at the end of the table. She shook her head. Ooops, I thought and took a deep breath. I consulted the glass in front of me and steadied myself. With the toast complete, the room took their seats and waited for the next toast. Looking around the room, I could see a couple of cadets had remained standing and grinning at each other from across the room. I recognized Logan at the far end of our table as he swayed and smiled at the people around him. The other cadet was KD and he stood merrily surveying the room from his spot halfway down the PMC's table.

"Ahh, the old last man standing," Olly said and passed the port.

The PMC looked at both of them disapprovingly. KD reached down and started to take his seat. Logan looked at him and waited until he fully seated before plonking down on his seat.

"Logan one, KD zero," I replied.

The Last Man Standing Game

Of all the games that are played at dining-ins, none is as elegantly simple as last man standing. After a toast is made, as the assembled diners take their seats, the player' simply stay standing for as long as they dare. With the whole mess seated, to remain standing draws the attention of the rest of the mess, including the Adjutant and Commanding Officer. The 'winner' is the one who stays standing the longest and whilst there no formal prize, you do get bragging rights at the bar afterwards. You are also likely to get a visit to the Adjutant's office on Monday for a bollocking and a few extras.

...

I couldn't remember how many toasts we had left and hoped we were almost done. Even though my vision had already started to swim, I could see that I wasn't the only one who was relieved when I heard the PMC excuse the mess for the bathroom break.

"Sheeeeeeeesh," said a disheveled looking Watts as he leant against the urinal.

"You can say that again," someone else said.

"Sheeeeeeesh," the big guy obligingly replied.

With bladders emptied and the formal part of the dinner over, we returned downstairs for the second-best part of the night. The formal guests were now able to leave, and this meant that all of the senior officers were out of the dining hall as we returned to our seats. A couple of the OC's had returned, and they looked like they were joining in with the spirit of the evening. The final part of the dining-in ritual was what we knew as The Kangaroo Court, which was a chance for the Corps to 'charge' their fellow classmates for misdemeanors that they felt others might have missed. Whilst there were no formal rules as to what the Kangaroo Court could hear, the 'charges' were generally kept to more lighthearted events. To start proceedings, the PMC took his place at the head of the table and called on the appointed members of the court to join him.

"Hear ye, hear ye. Court is now in session. Do we have any charges to be heard this evening?" he asked to the room as he topped up his port.

"Yes sir, we have a number," reported the 'prosecutor' who was seated beside him.

"Read the first charge," the PMC replied and lounged back in his chair.

The prosecutor stood up and pulled a folded set of notes from his jacket.

"I hereby call the defendant, Cadet Dansen from Kapyong company," he said aloud and surveyed the room.

Dansen stood up and braced himself up.

"Sir!"

The two cadets who had been appointed as the court's 'bailiffs', marched over to him and escorted him to the head table.

"It is hereby alleged that you have recently attempted to re-allocate yourself a new room in the lines and have been sleeping in the rec room. How do you plead?" the prosecutor said loudly, once he was in place.

"Not guilty Sir. You didn't see me do it, and you can't prove it," he replied with a grin.

"In which case, I call my first witness. Cadet Ryan, I believe you were the Duty Officer on Sunday after the last home rugby game," he said and looked around for Logan.

"Yes sir," Ryan said and stood up warily.

"Did you notice anything unusual when you were conducting your rounds on the Sunday morning in question?"

"I did. When assuming my duties, I noted a strange sound coming from the recreation room. At first, I thought someone was in there with a chainsaw, so I thought I would check. Upon further inspection,

I noted that cadet Dansen had assumed the prone unsupported position and was guarding the room with loud bursts of prolonged snoring," Ryan said.

"So, there you have it. I rest my case. You honor," the prosecutor said and bowed to the PMC.

"This looks like a clear case of portos-malfunction and this court finds you guilty as hell. You are hereby sentenced to three ports for your indecent assault on the ears of the company orderly," the PMC ordered.

"This is bullshit, your honor. But I will take your port from you, if you insist," Dansen said, to the cheers of the mess.

Three port glasses were filled and laid in front of him.

"One. Ha ha haa!" we all yelled as he emptied the first glass.

"Two. Ha ha haa!" as he emptied the second.

"Three. Ha ha haa!" as he slammed the third glass down in front of him and looked at us all through bleary eyes.

The court's powers were pretty limited, and most punishments were issued in a denomination of port skulls. Three was usually the minimum, although it could be reduced by an exceptional defense. Seven was regarded as the upper limit, as port had a nasty habit of repeating on you if you tried any more. Not that this stopped anyone. This often led to the mess gardens copping a plastering of foul smelling, purple liquid at some stage later in the night. A port spew was not something you forgot in a hurry, as the smell lingered with you for days after and was almost impossible to get out of your mess jacket. But we were expected to play as hard as we worked, and port was all part of the bargain. So, if you got challenged to down three, the natural response was to up the ante and make it five. Or six. Or seven.

We heard two more charges before being allowed to leave the dining room. One of the 1st class Cadets was given three for 'AWOL' after being accused of sleeping 'over the hill' during the week, whilst another was given five for an 'unauthorized discharge' after being caught taking a piss whilst on 'butts party'. The rest of us played along and cheered each time the punishments were announced. We spilled port on the tables as we attempted to fill our glasses in between charges. The remaining officers were as merry as the rest of us by the time the PMC called the dining-in to an end, and a few of us swiped the remining port decanters on the way out of the dining hall.

Olly and I rolled out of the dining hall with an arm over each other's shoulders and a decanter of half empty port between us. The final stage of any mess dinner took place in the bar area and it was the part of the night that most cadets looked forward to. Traditionally, an officer's mess should be the epitome of decorum and we were supposed to have our best manners on display. The only time the mess was allowed to actually be messy, was after a dining-in and only once the guests had left. This allowed the officers to blow off a bit of steam and enjoy themselves out of the prying eyes of the public and their senior officers. The PMC now handed his formal duties over to his deputy, who now assumed the responsibility for the running of mess games.

Over the years, these had changed, and would no doubt change again in the future, but they generally consisted of any combination of a number of basic drinking games that had evolved in the various messes over the years. The first was the age old 'boat race', which was pretty commonplace in most bars. The second was the 'obstacle race', which was a combination of physical exercises and drinking in teams. The obstacle course was made up of various props set up in the mess, where cadets had to dodge and weave their way through them and skull various concoctions along the way. Both of these had no prize, other than the glory your company claimed for winning.

The last, and most prized of games, was 'mess rugby'. Mess rugby was the name that had been given to a battle between two teams, dressed in their mess attire and pissed to the gills. It had the same basic concept as rugby, in that it had two teams and the goal was to put the 'ball' over the line, but that was about where it ended. The object was still to score the most points, but everything after that was pretty fuzzy. No halves were played, nor was the field marked. The 'ball' could consist of anything from one of the couch pillows to an old boot and any rules were pretty much ignored. It was a melee of the best sorts and one I never missed. The deputy PMC chose two teams arbitrarily and produced a frozen chicken that would be the ball for the game. A whistle was blown and that was about the last time we stopped for the next half an hour. We rucked, tackled, punched, gouged and rolled on the floor, trying to get the 'ball', or bits of it, over the line. Occasionally, it was deemed that one team had scored and the game was started again. At these breaks, we grabbed another beer and those who were wounded high-fived someone on the sideline to take their place. Shirts were ripped, noses bloodied, and bruises earned, but we didn't care. This mad-ape wrestling match was a chance for us to beat our chests and charge headlong into the fray alongside our mates. No-one would remember the score the next day, but they would remember who they battled alongside. It wasn't just the males, as there were plenty of females who were more than happy to tuck in. I remember looking across the field and seeing one of the girls come belting through the ruck and drop an elbow into the bloke holding a bit of frozen chicken. He went down like a sack of spuds and she pulled the chicken free before diving over the try line. The rest of the team cheered as she marched off to skull a beer and trade places with one of the by-standers.

At some stage near midnight, with our numbers reduced and the 'ugly' lights on, we were ushered out of the mess by the deputy PMC and the mess staff. We stumbled down the steps arm-in-arm, laughing and whooping into the night air. We zig-zagged our way around to the back of Kokoda and caged a couple of cigarettes off one of the cadets who was doing his best to keep from falling asleep in the garden. I'd managed to sneak out with a carafe of wine and pulled it out from under my mess jacket.

"I think I am officially drunk," said Olly as he leaned back against the wall of the company.

"Is that better or worse than being unofficially drunk?" I asked.

KD tried to spark up the lighter he'd borrowed as he squinted at the cigarette he was attempting to light.

"And I think KD is officially blind," I said and offered him the carafe.

"Piss off you lot, I'm the picture of sobriety," KD replied.

"Well, I hate to tell you this, but it's a pretty badly painted picture," Olly responded.

Even though it was heading towards spring, the night air was still chilly. If we were sober, we'd have headed for our warm rooms. But we had our 'rum blankets' on and no longer cared. On nights like these, the cold meant nothing, and tomorrow's hangover was too far away to think about. I looked around at Olly and KD, smiled and took a deep breath. As the night grew quiet around us, the old buildings no longer seemed cold, instead they felt warm and full of life. We were now part of their traditions and history, having earned our place over the course of the year.

KD's sleepy grin could be seen in the glow of his cigarette and I could see Olly smiling at something as he slumped back against the wall. The cold night air wrapped around us and we settled into the silence.

"Oi, don't go to sleep out here. You'll fucking freeze to death and I'm not hauling either of you inside," said KD moments later when he heard one of us start to snore.

We shook ourselves awake, not sure if he meant it or not. Knowing KD, he would leave us here too, just for a laugh.

"Righto, I'm going home," I slurred and staggered off towards my warm bed.

The others shook themselves off and headed off in their own directions. Tonight, we would all sleep soundly and would do our best to forget about tomorrow until we needed to.

The next morning as the sun blasted in through my window, I rolled out of bed groggily and tried to figure out what time it was. The OC had given us the morning off in place of the usual Saturday parade for a change. Possibly to avoid having to get up himself, as he looked like he was enjoying himself when I'd seen him. My head still throbbed, and I still had the lingering after-taste of mess port. I could feel a couple of sore spots on my elbows and under the ribs from mess rugby, but other than that, I seemed to be in one piece. I hadn't received a visit from the CSM and couldn't remember anyone telling me that I'd need to pay the OC a visit after the dining-in. Miracles do happen, I thought to myself.

After another hour of half-sleep, I made myself have a shower with the intent of rolling into town for a late breakfast. I found a couple of 3rd class cadets in the bathrooms when I got there and could see they'd been trying to clean up the mess that I could smell coming from somewhere. By the looks of it, one of their classmates had pulled a 'human hand-grenade'. They stopped briefly to make sure it wasn't the CSM and quickly resumed when they saw it was just me.

"One of you lot?" I asked.

"Not me, you know who," replied one of them and motioned in the direction of one of their mates who was looking pretty worse for wear.

"It happens. Make sure you give your mess jacket a good soak before you wash it, otherwise you'll never get the stains out," I offered and turned the shower on.

The rest of the weekend was uneventful as most of us were pretty hung over from the dining-in and were in no shape to back up on the Saturday night. Additionally, we knew that we had our final tactics assessment the next week and it was a 'must pass'. The assessment would be the planning of a company level defense and was not only a step up from everything we had done, it was also a level up from what we would be doing as young officers. Army soldiers and officers are expected to understand the roles above and below their ranks, in case the worst happened. Company level tactics were, in theory, much the same as platoon level tactics, except you had three times as many troops to manage. As such, your planning had to be more detailed, your understanding of your supporting capabilities (tanks, artillery, engineers) had to be greater, and your ability to read the ground had to be spot on. So, with the familiar pinks and greens scattered across the floor, we debated which part of the battlefield we offered the best tactical advantage during our evening study sessions. We no longer had to consult the pams for enemy weapon ranges or which symbols were needed to identify the separate elements of our forces on the map. These details were now part of our own internal pam, as they had been drilled into us time and time again throughout the year.

"Bullshit, the Mussorian platoons only have DSK's and RPG's, they'll never hit you from there," Watts offered.

"Get stuffed, of course they will. Check the distances on your map, numpty," Walker replied.

We argued late into the night as we scribbled in our note pads and marked up our maps. By now, these preparation activities had become routine and were nowhere as stressful as they had been in 2nd class. Tactics wasn't everyone's forte though, and each company had at least one or two who struggled with the complexities of putting together a battle plan. But, like everything else we did, we worked together to help out. Regardless of whether you were best mates or not, they were classmates. At least that was the way I thought about it, even though I knew there were still a few who were more interested in themselves than helping their classmates.

"What do you reckon the chances are that we'll get through?" Watts asked, as we finally started to throw our stuff back in well-worn ech-bags.

"Better than average. At least I hope so," I replied.

"As long as I don't get Schwartz as DS, I reckon I'm home," Hobbes chimed in with a wry smile.

"You and me both," I added.

"Well, I guess I'm in as well," Watts said.

"And we'll even throw in a set of steak knives," Hobbes added with a chuckle as we wandered off to our rooms.

After double-checking my TEWT gear, making sure I had a uniform ready and an alarm set, I flopped onto my bed. As I lay in my bed, the College was silent, and I tried to get my brain to process the details of the final assessment. Weapons ranges, enemy dispensation, fire support, possible formations, avenues of approach, DFs, LZs, FUPs and LDs swam through my head until I finally succumbed to sleep. As the gears in my mind slowly wound down, I slept as soundly as I ever had.

In between our other lessons, the PTI's still had plenty in store for us. Even though they knew us all by name and were never short of a joke when we trained, they didn't see the need to go easy on us. With graduation just around the corner, we were reminded that fitness was not an optional extra for young officers. By now the baby fat we'd carried when we arrived had disappeared, and we looked leaner, tougher. The color in our company PT shirts had faded and our runners were worn down to the soles. We charged through the obstacle course confidently, our rifles no longer finding soft spots to bite into when we dismounted from the ropes or flicked over the ten-foot wall. We pushed each other to see who could do the most push-ups, chin-ups and rope climbs. Our hands were callused from the old wooden 'heaving beams' that were now familiar friends. The PTI's requests for 'one more rep' were now met with a smile as we wrung the last ounces of strength from our weary muscles.

"Rickson, that's not the way you do it. Drop and give me twenty," Sergeant Tubbs said when he caught me jumping off the ten-foot wall.

Twenty press-ups? Anytime, I thought and dropped to the deck and threw my rifle over my shoulder.

"19, twenty, done," I grinned and jumped back to my feet.

"Well don't just stand there smart-arse, get going!" he yelled theatrically, pointing towards the next obstacle.

Clambering up to the top of the tower, I looked down at the faces my classmates and noticed how much they'd changed. In place of the fresh-faced individuals we were at the start of training, we now moved like the well-oiled machine we'd been drilled to be. We smiled and huddled closer to our teammates when the going got tough. Whether it was on the football field or the obstacle course, we learned the most important lesson that the College had to teach. As an individual, we could be skillful, fit and tactically sound, but the Army was a team sport, and we were now part of the team.

Lunch was a relaxed affair after the morning's PT session, and we took our time in the dining hall as we had nothing scheduled for the afternoon.

"What do you reckon the chances are that there will be a few re-tests on the final TEWT. I'm taking bets," Nathan announced from the end of the lunch table.

"It would have to be at least a dollar twenty for the exchange cadets. If you make it one fifty, I'll have twenty bucks," KD replied.

"You'd have to borrow the money to put that bet on," a voice from the table behind us offered.

"Piss off Bubski, you still owe me fifty bucks. Nathan, put me down for fifty and collect the money off him," KD said.

"What did you put in for your Corps selection?" Watts asked in between mouthfuls.

"Engineers or Trucks. I suppose you put Tanks then Tanks," I replied.

"Well, I'm not exactly built for walking and I like the idea of blowing things up."

"I did hear they a rumor that they've been looking at putting on bigger doors after they heard that you might be coming," I said with a grin.

"Get stuffed, you midgets are all the same. You'll thank me one day when I single headedly stop the Mussorian brigade dead in its tracks with my awesomeness."

"I'll buy you a beer when you do. But in the meantime, I better have a word to one of the blokes going to RAEME about boosting the suspension on those tanks too."

He offered me the finger in response. I gave him two back and we both grinned.

The next morning, we marched down to tactics wing for our final assessment with ech bags, fold up chairs and map boards tucked under our arms. The buses were already waiting for us when we arrived.

"On the bus!" Captain Lotterman yelled as he strolled down the hill with the rest of the DS.

The bus motors roared to life as we threw our gear into the storage bins. I made sure my bag was placed up against the back corner so it wouldn't fall out when we got there. I had added a couple of extras to my bag, as I was planning on celebrating once we were done. The buses lurched through the gears as we headed past the 'chicken on the stick' and the lake fountain. Most of us were jovial, but you could still see the odd nervous face looking out the window as we started to make our way out of town. We were headed for the rolling hills to the east of Canberra, where we would site our company position in an attempt to halt the advancing Mussorian brigades as they attempted to hit us from the west this time.

"If the bloody Mussorians have taken Sydney already, I reckon we'd be pretty stuffed. I don't know about you blokes, but I reckon about here is the time we call the Yanks in and just carpet bomb the shit out of 'em, Gulf war style," Logan offered.

"Now that is a set of orders I'll pay to hear," I replied.

"You reckon we could do that TEWT from inside the bus?" added KD.

"Don't you blokes ever learn? Never fight the green," there was always one spoilsport and this time it was Walker.

"Don't listen to him. Always fight wearing green, it matches with the rest of your outfit and is easy to keep clean," the Bensonhurst chipped in from the seat behind us.

The rest of us stifled a laugh and wondered exactly what was going on in his head.

Arriving at the TEWT site, I found myself assigned to Captain Lotterman's group and followed him over to a spot on the side of the hill for the initial briefs.

"All right, you know what you need to do. I'm going to be located under that tree right over there. Come and see me if you have any questions. My watch says, 0932. Back here on this spot at 1232. Off you go," he said and looked around the group to make sure we were paying attention.

He checked his watch again and sauntered off with his chair to find a shady spot. The rest of us scattered, looking for a decent spot to work from and make our mud-models. We spent the next hour scouting the ground around us, furiously scribbling on our maps. The DS wandered about and checked on our progress without being intrusive. There were no TEWT farms today, as the area was too big for us to cover on foot. We were still expected to be able to identify each position in detail, so we studied the ground carefully and double-checked our compass bearings. We were careful not to get caught standing too close to our classmates, in case the DS thought we were colluding (as we probably would have been). Luckily, the team from our company had been separated amongst the DS, as we had all come up with a similar solution during our late-night study session. Most of the TEWTs lent themselves to a couple of solutions, so it was likely that we'd present similar solutions during the brief.

I was still nervous as I finished scribbling the last bits of my plan in my field notebook and started to lay-out my mud-model. Seeing as it was our last TEWT, I thought I'd put in a bit of extra effort and had brought along a few additions to my standard kit. I carefully laid out plastic grid square markets and marked the north point with my bayonet. I was so engrossed in my model that I didn't hear Captain Lotterman approach.

"Interesting model Rickson, I'm hoping your solution is up to the same standard," he said.

He wandered around the rest of the group to see how they were progressing, occasionally stopping to make an observation or suggestion. After a full lap of the group, he pulled up at his chair and checked his watch.

"That's it everyone, time's up! Get in here," he yelled.

We quickly double-checked our models and made sure our briefs were in order. As I walked over, I saw the Possum fussing around with his model, still trying to finish the last touches.

"I said, time's up!" Captain Lotterman yelled, which got him moving.

With the group gathered around his chair, we waited nervously to find out who would be first. Lotterman went through the TEWT requirements and reminded us of the need for our solutions to be our own. He looked around for anyone who might be looking at the ground. We knew that if we looked too nervous, this would automatically result in being required to give the ground brief, so we each did our best to look confident and make eye contact as he scanned the group.

"Alright then. Rickson, you look like you're ready. You can be first," he said and pointed towards where I'd set up.

Beauty, I thought, at least I'd be put out of my misery quickly. By now, I was confident that I could in the very least write a passing ground brief, which would hopefully add to my chances of getting through.

"What the f..." I heard Logan whisper as he saw my creation.

"Jesus, you have way too much spare time on your hands," added KD and shook his head.

I smiled, hoping the rest of the group enjoyed my handiwork. I fished an old ski pole out of my ech-bag and pointed to the bayonet.

"Ladies and gentlemen, please orientate your maps. This is the north point," I began.

There was a small Santa sitting on the end of the bayonet, in what I thought would be an obvious reference to north. Our forces were made up of a small Star Wars figures, augmented by a mobile force of matchbox cars. Small plastic cows and sheep roamed around the map, along with a farmer's tractor. The enemy was made up of a convoy of black plastic spiders and the artillery markers were plastic flags with 'bang' written on them.

"This had better be good," Captain Lotterman said and folded his chair out.

I pulled out my field message notebook and cleared my throat.

"It will be Sir. Prepare to copy everyone," I replied with a smile.

I rushed through the brief, hoping that I'd interpreted the pinks and greens properly. It wasn't fantastic, but Lotterman nodded and let me move through the rest of the plan quickly. My plan to crush the spider army by holding them in place on the highway and flank them with my armoured force was deemed workable. With modifications. In my haste and overconfidence, I'd forgotten a few details, but I could tell by the look on Captain Lotterman's face that I'd got through.

"Ok. Next – Cadet Logan."

And as simply as that, I'd passed my final assessment. It all seemed a bit easy and I wondered if Captain Lotterman knew what he had just done. Like the final move in a game of chess, it was subtle yet decisive. Passing tactics had just granted me a ticket out of the College. As I walked over to the next mud-model, I grinned and tried not to get too excited. The rest of the group seemed to get through, albeit with a few pointed comments to illustrate that we still had plenty to learn. Once the last set of orders was complete, the final brief from Captain Lotterman seemed to fly by and before we knew it, we were sitting in the shade waiting for the buses.

"Jesus boys, I think we might have almost made it," I said.

"Don't get ahead of yourself, you'll think of some way to stuff up between now and graduation parade," KD replied.

"Possibly, but I reckon even I'd have my work cut out for me to stuff up that badly."

"Well, knowing you, I reckon you could come up with something," Logan added with a sly grin.

We nodded in agreement and chuckled, knowing he was actually right.

With the hands on my watch clicking over to read 1600, we finally piled off the buses outside the main lecture hall. Before being dismissed, we were gathered together on the kerb for one final brief from Captain Schwartz.

"Well done cadets, you have passed the last of your tactics assessments and I congratulate you on getting this far in your training. Once you leave here you will be required to put what you have learned into practice and continue to hone your skills as you progress throughout your career. For those of you lucky enough to be heading to the infantry, this is only the first step in your tactical journey as you still have your regimental training to get through before you will be entrusted in leading soldiers in the field. Remember, as long as you are leading soldiers, your training will never stop," he said sternly and paused to look at us.

"But for now, you can congratulate yourselves on a job well done. Good luck for the rest of your careers, I'm sure it won't be too long before we bump into each other again."

Whilst it sounded like a pre-recorded message, we could see plenty of smiles amongst the DS and they shook our hands before we headed back to the lines. As I was turning to leave, Captain Schwartz tapped me on the shoulder.

"Yes Sir?" I said as I turned to face him.

"Rumor has it that you're going to Transport."

"Seems that way, Sir," I replied.

"And why the hell would you do that? You know that you'd be happier in the infantry, don't you?"

"Maybe, but I reckon I'm better suited to being in the rear with the gear, Sir. Who knows, I might even be able to help you out with a ride someday," I said with a grin.

"Well, I'm sure we'll catch up somewhere. But for now, I'm sure there's a beer with your name on it at the bar. Get out of here."

"You're not lying there, Sir. I reckon there's probably at least a half dozen!"

At the mess bar that afternoon the mood was jubilant. The bar heaved with bodies as it seemed like the entire class had managed to squeeze their way into the mess. I tried to convince the PMC to shout the bar, with no luck. He pointed out that if anyone was going to be shouting the bar, it should probably be me. I didn't disagree and reached up to ring the bell at the end of the bar.

"Drinks are on me!" I proclaimed to the cheers of my classmates.

The gathered mass surged towards the bar in a wave of bodies. I paused briefly to consider whether it was a good decision before someone shoved a beer in my hand.

"I reckon we're almost done brother," Watts said as he threw an arm around my neck.

"You'll be done if you keep up this rate," I replied.

"Illegitimi non carborundum, my friend," he grinned and raised his glass.

Outside the daylight slowly started to disappear as the sounds of the celebration leaked out into the night air. Beers were eventually traded for rum and then much, much later for the mess port. I remember crawling out of the room-in-a-room at some stage later that night before the rum fairy spirited me back to my room and left me slumbering soundly, still in my uniform.

With all of our assessments now complete, all that was left was getting through parade practice and the necessary administration that would get us from the College to our first postings. During the day we lounged casually in our chairs as we listened to briefings about what we needed to do as soon as we marched into our new units. We spent the evenings writing letters to our new commanding officers and worked on getting our parade uniforms ready. I'd been successful in my application to Transport and intended on trying to secure a posting to one of the road transport units up north. In comparison to everything else we did at the College, sorting out our postings was oddly simple. Most followed the advice of their career advisor or tried to get a posting close to their family. Even though the Army thought of us as young officers, we were still kids at heart and most of us liked the idea of being close to some sort of family if we could. I hadn't lived at home since I was fifteen and the closest place to a home that I knew was Darwin. This turned out to be lucky as my fellow 'truckies' were more than happy to let me take the slot available up there.

With that out of the way, the only thing left for us to do now was to get through the long days of drill practice that were necessary to make graduation parade run smoothly. Even though the format of the parade was exactly the same, we went over it again and again and again, until the drill staff were satisfied that we met their standards. The drumbeats echoed off the buildings as we marched onto the parade ground with the Drilly's chasing behind us. We rounded the parade ground in slow and quick time, making sure we swung around 'like a gate' at each of the corners. Our free arms punched their way up to shoulder height, while we locked our rifles in by our side with the other one. We slid to a halt and snapped our rifles up to the attention position time and time again, until the Drilly's were satisfied that we were all moving in unison.

Each time we'd march off, we'd be reminded to hydrate and stay out of the sun. By now the Canberra summer had started to flex its muscles and by mid-morning the parade ground felt like you were standing on a hotplate. Allow yourself to get dehydrated and you were almost guaranteed to bacon. So, we continuously drank from our luke-warm water bottles as we stood around under the trees during the breaks. As expected, the week got off to a slow start as we slowly switched our bodies and minds back into drill mode. We were rusty on Monday, and Tuesday was marginally better, even though we still ended up on the square for the better part of two hours. For some reason Wednesday's session was scheduled straight after lunch, which would coincide with the parade ground reaching maximum temperature. As we formed up in front of the company, I could already see the heat shimmering off the parade ground.

"Bloody hell, this is not going to be fun," Watts said, beads of sweat already forming on the back of his shirt.

"Head up big guy, you might be the first bacon for the week," I replied and slapped him on the back.

"Nah, rumor has it that the blokes from Kapyong were on the piss last night. My money is on one of them," Hobbes chimed in.

Even though we were allowed off barracks whenever we didn't have programmed lessons, it was a big call to get on the piss mid-week. Especially when you knew you had drill practice in the afternoon. The Long Tan lads had snuck out for a couple on Monday night, but we could see the double drill practice on our calendar for Wednesday and opted to stay in on Tuesday. Now that he'd mentioned it, I remembered seeing Matt and Rob at breakfast that morning. Both had glassy eyes and still smelt like rum. They were going to be in the hurt locker if we got stuck out there for the full two hours.

"Company attennnn-shun!" the CSM yelled and we snapped our heels together.

"Wake up you lot! That sounded like gunfire, everyone together, listen to the words of command. CSM, do it again," Sergeant Ruth commanded, his voice bouncing off the surrounding buildings.

I hoped that this was not a bad omen. Afternoon drill sessions were often a bit of a cluster as everyone was a bit slow after morning activities and a lunch.

"Long Tan Company... Atten-shun!" the CSM yelled.

We were better this time, but still a long way off where we needed to be. Sergeant Ruth walked along the ranks, adjusting spacing and reminding us to straighten ourselves up. Like a cattle-dog, he moved quickly and barked where he needed to as we marched around to the parade ground.

"This is going to be a long afternoon," Watts whispered from behind me.

After slotting ourselves into the rest of the companies, we relaxed and chatted as we waited for the band to arrive. I looked across at the boys from Kapyong and could see a couple of them passing a bottle of water between them.

"Has that got any rum in it, or is that coming out of your skin?" I yelled over to them.

"All bourbon, no coke. That's how tough I am," replied Cook with one of his trademark grins. The big guy stood well over six feet and his red face stood out above the rest of the cadets around him. Amongst his many talents, he was known for his ability to sweat continuously and I could see he wasn't looking forward to the next couple of hours.

"I've got you at short odds Cook, don't let one of these other bastards beat you," I said.

"You'll lose that money every day of the week. If you want to make some money, I'd say Matt is the favorite after last night."

I could see Matt leaning against one of the buildings, shaking his head. He'll be pushing it to get through the first run through, I thought.

"Corps!" yelled the DWSM from his position at the edge of the parade ground.

We quickly shuffled back into formation and readied ourselves.

"Corps by the left! Band by the center! Quuuuuuuick – march!"

The snare drums of the band rattled away in quick bursts, with the bass drum marking time behind them. On cue, we stepped off and marched in procession onto the parade ground. The Drilly's marched behind each company, reminding us to swing our arms to the proper height and keep ourselves aligned with the markers. The heat coming off the parade ground felt like I was standing inside an oven. With no breeze and no shade, it was going to be a long two hours. The parade usually took about thirty minutes to get through without any speeches or inspections, but that would depend on how many stuff-ups we had in between. The DWSM peppered us with comments from his position at the front of the parade ground and there were no doubts as to when we didn't get it right.

"What the hell are you lot doing?! Swing it around like a gate and dress off the right marker!"

"That was uniformly terrible. We are going to be here all afternoon!"

"Bloody hell, my ninety-year-old grandmother could do a better job than you lot!"

We practiced the march past three times in slow time and twice in quick time. I could feel the sweat starting to pool on my back as we practiced our salutes over and over again. From the corner of my eye, I could see Watts start to sway at the end of the rank. I knew he would be sweating buckets and each minute in the heat put him one step closer to going over.

"Wiggle your toes and breathe," Sergeant Ruth reminded everyone as we stood silently, awaiting the inspection that would normally occur at this stage of the parade.

We remained at attention, chests held high and shoulders back. My rifle sling steadily bit into my shoulder and the soles of my feet burned inside my boots. I forced myself to breathe deeply and worked on trying to flex my thigh muscles to keep the blood moving. The BSM and DWSM slowly walked through the ranks, pausing occasionally to say something to one of the cadets.

"Eh CSM, what's the chances we can give the inspection a miss today?" Hobbes whispered.

"Yeah, and the rest of the march off too. Just tell 'em we're good for it and we'll make it up in our own time," I added with a chuckle.

"Shut-up you two," Ruth hissed from behind us.

One of the things we learned from drill practice is how to look out of the corners of your eye. This is used most to keep yourself in line with the rest of the rank, but it also came in handy to work out where the inspecting officer was and how long you had to go. As per the rest of our formal parades, the inspecting officer would be accompanied by the BSM, and they would walk through a rank of each company to conduct a quick inspection. This involved stopping to speak briefly to one of the cadets in each company, before returning to the dais and giving a speech. For our regular parades the inspection party was usually the CO and Adjutant. On occasion, the Commandant would make an appearance, but it was rare. For graduation, we would have the Commandant and the Governor General. The inspection process usually took about five minutes but could take longer if the reviewer wanted to take their time. As we stood to attention and waited, the effects of the heat started to kick in. Once your blood pressure started to drop, if you didn't get moving quickly there was a good chance that you'd wake up on the tarmac. For some reason the BSM was held up at Kokoda company and I could see a couple of the junior cadets in front of me start to sway. I was so focused on them that I didn't catch the movement out of the corner of my eye until I heard the rifle clatter against the bitumen. It wasn't Watts, but one of the 3rd class blokes at the end of my rank. I could make out his crumpled form on the parade ground and heard Sergeant Ruth march around to where he lay.

"Head and eyes to the front, the rest of you. Keep moving your feet in your boots and for God's sake, keep breathing," he hissed.

After what felt like an hour, the BSM finally called us to attention and we closed ranks in readiness for the march-off. On the march back to the company, I could see the dark lines of sweat on the backs of the cadets in front of me. Sergeant Ruth had retrieved the young bloke who'd gone down, and he stood gingerly under one of the trees waiting for us.

"Company. Fall, out!" the CSM ordered after we'd halted in front of the lines.

"Thank fuck for that," Hobbes said from behind me.

"You can say that again," Watts said and wiped the sweat off his brow.

"Thank fuck for that," Hobbes said.

Our faces were red from our efforts and our foreheads bore the imprints of the stitching from our slouch hats. But we'd made it one day closer to graduation and that was all that mattered.

As the second Tuesday in December drew near, parents and friends started to arrive from across the country. As soon as we were finished each day, we'd race off into town to see them. Inevitably, we'd bump into a few of our classmates with their parents or girlfriends as they did the rounds of local restaurants and pubs. With one day until graduation, I found myself sharing a beer in the Olim's beer garden with a handful of mates and their parents.

"Well, I must say, I'm proud of you for sticking with it. There were a few times that I wasn't sure if we were going to be here in December," my dad said quietly as sat.

"Just goes to show, miracles do happen," I replied with a grin.

"Well, whatever it took, I'm glad we're almost done. I can't wait to get out of here," Watts said from his seat beside me.

"That makes three of us. I thought I was never going to get out of the place," Hobbes chimed.

"Well, I couldn't have done it without you blokes. You know what it's like. There were plenty of times that I was ready to pack it in, jump in the truck and hit the road," I said and aimed my glass at them.

"Shit, there's plenty of days I still feel like that. Next time you're thinking of packing it in, give me a yell!" Watts replied with one of his big grins.

We sat around in the late afternoon sun joking about life after graduation and how long it would take before we would up on someone's shit list when we got to our units. We knew that even though our time at the College was almost done, we still had a long way to go until would be allowed to command troops or call ourselves leaders. But we knew we were a step closer and felt that if we could get this far, then we could make through whatever else the Army had in store for us after graduation.

Waking up in my room the next morning, I peeled the curtains open to reveal dawn's early light as it started to creep across the sky. The birds called to each other in the trees outside my window. For a change, the sense of uneasiness that I'd felt every day since marching over the hill had disappeared and I felt at peace. I slowly threw my legs over the bed and rubbed my face with my hands. In the hallway, I could hear the occasional door open and close as the rest of the company started to come alive. In the distance I could hear the Duty Officer preparing the flag party as the rest of the College started the new day. The mood at rollcall was buoyant. We joked and grinned stupidly as Vinny read the roll. I could see that even the 3rd class cadets felt it, for they had also made it through their initial hurdles and had earned their place in 2nd class. The 2nd class cadets were also quietly happy as they knew they would take our places at the end of the parade. They would assume their new ranks tomorrow and, on the weekend, they would take our places at the bar.

"Jeez, you'd be glad getting out of here today, wouldn't you?" said the fresh-faced 3rd class cadet whose room was next to mine.

"I'm not so sure, I was thinking I might stick around for another six months. I'm just beginning to enjoy this place," I replied with a wink.

"I doubt it, not even you are that stupid," said Hobbes from the hallway as he rushed past on his way to the showers.

"Don't tempt me!" I shouted after him and offered a two fingered salute.

With the sun stretching it's golden fingers across the company buildings and parade ground, the College started to stretch and flex beneath us. As it came to life, it eyed us knowingly and nodded its weary head to let us know we had earned its respect. Its job done, it now turned its attention to those that remained and grinned in anticipation of the challenges that it had in store for them. For those about to graduate, we had now earned its respect and it added our names to the list of those who had passed the tests necessary to be considered junior officers.

After breakfast we went about the business of doing our final uniform checks and getting our gear ready for the evening's celebration. Even though the parade was our last official duty, we didn't officially graduate until midnight. Once the parade was finished, we would still have weapons to return and a handful of final signatures left on our march-out paperwork. We frantically checked our gear to make sure we had everything on the list as rumor had it that you wouldn't be allowed to leave if you hadn't completed your sign-off sheet. For a change, all of us took this admin seriously, so we scrambled around making sure we had everything in order. After a year of training almost all of us had lost a couple of issued items. As a result, we kept little stashes of extra gear just in case we'd need them. Where we didn't have something, we begged and borrowed from the 2nd and 3rd class cadets in our company, with promises we'd make it up at some stage. Over the years, I was sure that there were plenty of items that were never found and simply remained lost in time. As each class passed out, the next class assumed their debts, which they in turn passed on to the class below them. These little favors were as much a part of cadet life as anything else, as we knew they'd be repaid one day. Not everyone shared this view, but the number of jack cadets was always less than the number of good hands, and these traditions continued year after year. After a year of ROPs, show parades and plenty of extras, I was actually the most squared away, much to the shock of many of my classmates.

"Hey, you wouldn't have a spare filter would you," Vinny asked.

"You bloody Fijians are hopeless, why can't you keep your shit together?" I replied with a grin.

"It's not my fault man, I lost it in 3rd class," he said and held up his hands.

"Well, you might be in luck as I think I have two. What's it worth?" I replied and dug into my pack.

"You're a champion! I'll buy you a beer tonight," he grinned.

"Make it two and you've got a deal," I said, holding the filter up.

"Done!" he replied and snatched it out of my hands.

By mid-morning, the temperature had started to climb, and it looked like we would be in for a cracking day. Knowing we'd be on the parade ground for a while, I chugged on a bottle of water as I gave my gear one final check. For once, we'd headed home early the night before and I silently thanked myself for showing a bit of restraint. Heading out onto the parade ground with a solid hungover would have been tough. Given how many people would be watching the parade, a bacon today would be something that you would never live down. Especially if it was your own graduation parade. I gave my brass a quick wipe down and dabbed at a couple of spots on my parade boots, until I was finally satisfied that everything was as good as it could be. With twenty minutes to go until the parade started, I got dressed and unlocked my rifle from its rack. I placed my rifle on my desk and double-checked that the magazine was securely in place and the sling buckle was locked tight. I tucked and folded my parade jacket under my belt, before throwing my rifle over my shoulder. Looking in the mirror, I placed my blues cap on my head and made sure it was straight. Lastly, I grabbed my white gloves and room key off the table.

"Almost done mate," I said to myself in the mirror with a wink and walked out into the hallway.

The rest of the company was already in front of the company by the time I got down the stairs. They checked each other over for fluff, gave their brass final polishes and made sure their belts were in the right position. Sergeant Ruth and Captain Yeoman were also there, and they grinned as they watched us.

"Company!" the CSM yelled.

The company turned to face her and braced up.

"Sir, Long Tan company is assembled," the CSM said and saluted the OC.

Captain Yeoman returned the salute and turned towards us. He paused to scan the ranks with a steely gaze before speaking.

"Thank you CSM, at ease everyone," he said.

"Today is a good day. For today, we salute the 1st class cadets who have made it through their training and are now ready to take the next steps towards becoming junior officers. To you I say, congratulations. To the rest of the company, today is also an important day, as you have now completed the next stage of your training. Well done, but the battle is not over for you, so do not drop your bundles just yet. Let's have a good show on parade, show the rest of the Corps what Long Tan is made of. Sergeant Ruth."

"Sir!" Sergeant Ruth said and saluted.

After returning the salute, Captain Yeoman gave us one final look and marched off toward the parade ground.

"Righto you lot, you heard the OC. We've got one final parade to get through today, so let's make it a good one. Looking at the crowd, I can see plenty of mums and dads out there. All looking very proud and looking forward to a good show. So, let's switch on and keep switched on, until we are back here at the end of the parade. Don't embarrass yourselves and don't embarrass the CO. That is all," he said and looked over at the CSM.

"Company! Let's get this show on the road," the CSM said, as a broad grin spread across her face.

We shuffled ourselves into ranks, careful not to tread on each other's parade boots. As we stood shoulder to shoulder ready for the command to get going, I felt a tap on my shoulder and looked around to see Sergeant Ruth standing behind me.

"About time you got out of here, even you can't fuck up badly enough not to graduate from here," he whispered with a smile.

"I could give it a go," I replied.

"No, you fucking won't. You've finally learned to play the game, so get out there and finish it," he said and nodded towards the parade ground.

He was right, not even I could screw up from here. I looked out towards the parade ground and grinned in anticipation.

"Corps, by the left. Band, by the Centre. Quuuuuuuuuicckkk... March!" the RSM called from his position at the front of the parade ground.

The snare drums rolled, and the bass drum thumped. On cue, the Corps stepped off like a giant centipede. Left, right, left, we whispered to ourselves, as our boots kept in time with the drum beat. The crowd clapped as each company made their way onto the parade ground. I thought I could make out my parents amongst the crowd as we marched to our position in the middle of the parade ground. We wheeled around and halted, our movements precise and snappy. We saluted the colors as they were marched on before opening ranks to wait for the inspection. We wriggled our feet in our boots and flexed the muscles as the reviewing officer inspected the troops. The sun was high in the sky by now and the temperature was well on its way to the high twenties. I listened out for the telltale sound of a bacon in the ranks and was pleased when I didn't hear any. The reviewing party arrived at the end of our rank and we braced ourselves a little more in readiness. I could hear them talk quietly as they walked along the rank and was surprised when they stopped in front of me. The BSM motioned toward me and said, "This is Staff Cadet Rickson, who is one of our graduating class."

"Sir," I replied.

"And how have you found the training?" asked the reviewing officer.

"Excellent Sir," was all I could think of.

"And where are you off to next?"

"Darwin Sir."

"Well, it'll be hot up there. I hope you enjoy the heat. Well done," he responded politely, before continuing his inspection.

The RSM gave me a sly grin and shook his head as he walked past.

"I bet that's the first time you got to speak to the PM," whispered Hobbes out of the corner of his mouth.

He was right, as the reviewing officer for our parade had turned out to be the Prime Minister and he was also right, in that it would be the first and last time I'd ever get to speak to him. We all grinned and relaxed a little, as the inspection finished. I could feel the sweat starting to drip down by back as I listened to the speeches and hoped they didn't drag on for too long. After the final salutes were given, the moment we had been working towards and waiting for all year finally arrived.

"Graduating class!" the BSM called from his position at the front of the parade ground.

The 1st class cadets stepped out of the ranks and marched out to the front of the parade. The rest of the parade re-joined ranks in a series of precise maneuverers that could only be achieved on a military parade ground as the crowd clapped loudly.

"Graduating class, by the left. Quuuuuiiiick," the BSM ordered.

The snare drums rolled again, and the bass drum echoed behind. At the commencement of the third drum roll, we stepped off for our final lap of the parade ground. Heads held high and backs straight, it was without a doubt the happiest moment I'd ever had on a parade ground. As we rounded the final turn, I recalled all of the times I'd wearily plodded the same path in the early morning fog in full marching gear. I couldn't help but smile as I remembered all of the show parades, stoppage of leave parades and extras that I'd done. The mood in the ranks was quietly jubilant as we marched along the rear of the parade ground and listened for the BSM's final commands.

"Graduating Class, halt!" the BSM commanded.

Our parade boots scraped the bitumen briefly before slamming into the ground as one.

"Graduating Class, left turn."

We pivoted in positions to turn back towards the parade ground as the audience proudly looked on from the stands. Even the BSM had managed to crack a smile as he stood in front of us.

"Graduating Class. Faaaaaaallllll out!"

In unison we turned to our right and took three steps before exploding into whoops and hollers. Our parade caps flew into the air as we hugged and high-fived each other. I pulled my hat off my head and tucked it under my arm as I took the moment in. In the background we could hear the cheers of the crowd as the rest of the parade started to mobilize for their departure.

"Maaaaaaaaaate, how good is this!?!?!" Watts yelled at me as he picked me up in a bear hug.

"Not bad at all, my friend. Not fucking bad at all," I replied and gave the top of his head a kiss.

After a few minutes of slapping each other on the back, hugging and high-fiving, hats were returned to heads and we marched off in company groups. On the march back to the lines you could feel the energy in the air as the adrenaline continued to flush through our systems. We smiled and laughed as we covered the short distance back to Long Tan. Arriving at the company, we found our parents and friends standing out front, pride and joy evident on their faces. My mother greeted me with the biggest smile I think I'd ever seen and threw her arms around me.

"You made it!" she said.

Around me, other parents did the same as they hugged sons and daughters. Tears flowed and smiles could be seen on every face.

"I guess this means I'm going to have to pay up on all those bets that the Drilly's made on you not making it," grinned the CSM as she walked past.

"You're kidding, aren't you? I was a dead cert!" I replied.

"A definite maybe, at best," she said and shook her head.

We moved out of the way as the rest of the company marched their way back to the lines. Once they'd fallen out, we shook hands with the rest of the company and offered them our congratulations now they had made it one step closer to making it through. Now that we were finished, they would assume the responsibility of maintaining the traditions of the College and day to day running of the Corps. After midnight, we would only be memories, as the next class stepped into our place and forged their own paths towards graduation.

"Righto, you lot. Stop lolly-gagging about and get those rifles into the armoury," Sergeant Ruth called, triggering us to get moving.

With my rifle finally secured in the armoury, I felt naked as I marched back to the lines. Across the Corps, the sounds of blaring stereos and busy bodies echoed off the buildings. The remaining cadets still had jobs to do and turned their focus to the next stretch of their training. As they bustled about to the noise of slamming of doors and thumping feet in the hallways, I was at peace in my own little bubble, content I had done my part and that the College had no more in store for me.

By the time I'd got back to my room, all I wanted to do was put my feet up and carefully hung my parade uniform up before lying on my bed. As I lay there, the events of the year ran through my head. I smiled as I recalled each of the various tests, exercises and parades that the year had thrown at us. Even though I knew they were only a steppingstone to what would come next, I felt proud of having got through and smiled as each event ran through my mind.

After lying there for a while, I dragged myself back to reality and chucked on some civvies. My dinner jacket and uniform were already laid out on my desk, along with a set of lieutenants pips that we would be allowed to wear at midnight. I bundled the rest of my uniform into my ech-bag before throwing the lot over my shoulder and heading out to the carpark. On the way to town, all I could think about was a couple of cold beers and the chance to relax for a couple of hours before Graduation Party.

"Hey, here he is!" my dad shouted as I opened the door to the apartment.

I hung my gear on the back of a chair and twisted the top off the beer he handed to me.

"Cheers everyone," I said to the room full of people.

Glasses were raised as a cheer went up around the room. Besides my family, Watts and Walker had joined me as their families were staying over the other side of town. The atmosphere inside the small apartment was electric, music played on the stereo and my dad kept making rounds of the room to make sure everyone's drink was full. My parents listened intently as we told them stories about each of the years events and roared with laughter. A few times I saw them looking at each other and shaking their heads. We pressed on regardless and by the time we were ready to head back to the College our faces were glowing with excitement.

"The taxi will be here in fifteen minutes. You lot had better get your gear on," dad yelled.

In unison, we checked our watches before bolting off to find where we'd left our uniforms. Even with a couple of drinks under our belt, we were still able to manage the split in under ten minutes.

"Don't forget your pips!" I reminded the others as we hastily threw our jackets on.

"Shit, has anyone got any spares?" Watts said.

"You've got to be f-ing kidding," Walker said.

"I know they're here somewhere," Watts replied as he rummaged through his ech-bag.

"I think I might have a couple spare," I said and went to look.

"Found them!" Watts yelled triumphantly, as he held them aloft.

"Jesus mate, here I was thinking that I'd be the one not making it to midnight," I said and punched him in the shoulder.

"We're not there yet..." Walker said from behind me.

"Well, cross your fingers and count the hours," I replied and downed the remnants of my beer.

By the time we got there, the mess was heaving cadets and their guests. People spilled out of the mess bar and a steady buzz of conversation filled the air. As we moved through the mess, we introduced our parents to the various staff and instructors while trying to contain our excitement and keep a straight face. I think the CO was surprised I actually had parents when I introduced him to them. Always the picture of military professionalism, he was polite and aloof, in the manner we had grown used to. He knew that while this was a big step for us, it was only the first step towards the rest of the challenges that the Army had in store for us. Captain Yeoman seemed amused when I introduced him to my parents and told my dad that he was pleasantly surprised when he found out that I'd made it. The look my dad gave me reminded me that I had possibly left out a number of details in my regular updates. He took it in his stride and laughed along, but I could see that I would have to explain a few things to him later.

The rest of the night was a blur, as we lost, then found, and then lost our families and friends in our haste to make sure we had a drink with everyone in the class. Finally, with the midnight hour almost upon us, we formed up in the main foyer and waited for the clock to chime. A great cheer went up through the building as the mess clock started to ring in the new day. Friends and family gathered around as we attempted to put the pips of a junior officer on our uniform. We struggled with the fiddly little prongs, trying to punch them through the heavy cotton of our mess jackets. More than a few ended up broken and most of them ended up a bit crooked, but they were on and that was all that mattered. I remember my grandmother looking at me through misty eyes as she hugged me and smiled.

"Your grandfather would have been very, very proud," she said into my ear and I realized that the journey that I'd undertaken had not only been for myself. I'd gotten so caught up in my own battles, that I had forgotten that I was also representing my family, in particular those of my relatives who had served previously. None of my relatives were decorated war heroes or great commanders, but they had done their time respectfully and now I was the next one in line.

I don't know what time I got home, but I woke up still wearing my mess trousers and a very stained white dress shirt. Looking around, I realized I had made it back to the apartment somehow. The benches were still covered in empty beer bottles from the revelry of the night before. My mouth tasted foul and I tentatively sniffed my mess jacket to see if I could ascertain what we'd been drinking. The series of dark stains down the front of it said rum and coke, but there was an underlying smell of liquorice that said the ouzo had been out again.

"Bloody hell, Walker..." I muttered and looked around for a clean glass.

The sound of a flushing toilet told me I wasn't the only one awake and moments later Watts's disheveled face appeared around the corner.

"Good night, eh?" he said and collapsed on the couch.

"I think so. Looks like we made it home in one piece at least. Where's Walker?" I asked.

"Isn't he here?" Watts said from where he lay on the couch.

"Don't think so, I vaguely remember him trying to impress one of the Moose barmaids at some stage," I replied.

We chatted for a while until I figured I was sober enough to drive. I contemplated having a shower, before deciding I'd rather just get back to the lines to sort out the last of my admin. We organized to meet up for lunch and I stumbled out the door to try and remember where I'd left my car.

Back at the lines, the company was a hive of activity as the end of-class room moves took place. I'd already handed back most of my gear during the week and only had one drop off to make, so I was in no hurry. After a long hot shower and shave, I slipped into a set of acceptable civvies and headed down to the OC's office. I expected there to be a line up to get our final signature off the OC, but somehow no one else was there.

"Morning Sir," I said as I knocked on his door.

"Come on in," Captain Yeoman replied in his usual relaxed tone.

Out of habit, I marched in and braced up in front of his desk.

"Just here to get your signature Sir," I said, standing at attention.

"Relax, you're not a cadet anymore. Grab a seat," he said, motioning to the seat behind me.

I pulled the chair over and sat down.

"How did you pull up this morning?" he asked, leaning back in his chair.

"Not bad... I've been worse. Sir," I replied.

"Well, you're in one piece and you have now, somehow, managed to graduate. You know, when I picked up the OC's job, the first thing the old OC gave me was your file," he said and picked up what must have been my personnel file. The folder budged with loose notes and I could also make out the folded yellow charge sheet that stuck out of the sides.

"Yes, Sir," I replied and tried to look earnest.

"Now, I have to say, I don't think I've seen this many disciplinary notes in the one place. So, as you could imagine, I didn't hold much hope for your chances in getting out of here."

We both looked at the bulging folder on his desk in silence.

"Somehow you did though. I know Sergeant Ruth had a few words to you along the way, but at the end of the day, you pulled your shit together and did it. I didn't think I was going to say this, but congratulations," he said and offered his hand over the desk.

I stood up, smiled and shook his hand.

"Thanks Sir, appreciate it."

"But, before you go, I've got a bit of advice for you. I can see that you're the sort of guy that likes to question things and push the envelope a bit, which I understand. After all, it wasn't so long ago that I was in your place and I remember being young and dumb enough to think that I knew better. However, let me tell you this. As a junior officer, the soldiers in your unit will be watching what you do. If they see you trying to buck the system, they will do the same. Your peers know how you feel but have learned how the system works and why it's important to stick to the game plan. If you're going to do any good as a Lieutenant, you need to understand that your first job is to follow your bosses lead. At all times. When you're on the piss with your mates, you can do what you want. But in the barracks and in the field, set the standard that you want your soldiers to follow. Am I getting through to you?" he said and sat up in his chair.

"Yes, sir. Loud and clear," I replied.

"Alright then, give us that bit of paper and let's get you out of here," he said.

"Thanks Sir," I said and passed him my march-out paperwork.

"Now, one last thing," he said as he handed the paperwork back to me.

"Yes, sir."

"What the hell were you thinking going to trucks? You would have been a hell of a lot happier in the infantry," he said with a grin.

"Well, you know what they say, Sir. A second-class ride's better than a first-class walk!"

I could see him shaking his head as I walked into the hallway.

I spent the next couple of hours stuffing gear into my car and checking off the list of things we had to do before we left. It felt a bit surreal and I kept thinking that one of the instructors would turn up at some stage and tell us all that we still had one more test to pass. As I passed my classmates, I could see a few of them thinking the same thing as they walked around the company cautiously. I knew I would be seeing some of them soon as we'd be classmates again on our next courses, whilst the rest I'd likely to run into again on exercise or in barracks somewhere in the future.

"You almost done in here, Sir?"

It was the 2nd class cadet who was moving into my room and he stood at the doorway with his pack over his shoulder.

"All yours mate, be kind to it," I said and tossed him the keys.

"Any stains I need to avoid?" he asked.

"Nah, you're safe in here. This is a frat-free zone."

"Sweet, I can't guarantee that it will stay that way," he replied with a wink.

"I'll leave that up to you and as parting gifts, I've left you my afro wig, some spare talc's, my notes on defensive ops and half a bottle of port. Go forth and multiply, young cordy," I said and dropped the keys on the table.

I helped him drag his trunk in from the hall and we shook hands before I headed down the hall to see if I could catch a few classmates one last time. Down the hall, Vinny was still sweating and swearing in his room, as he tried to shove all of his remaining clothes into a tattered old suitcase.

"Need a hand?" I asked.

"Nah, I'm good. I don't know where all of this extra stuff came from," he said and wiped his brow.

"I bet it's full of underwear from all of the university girls you've been seeing," I offered with a grin.

"Jesus, I wish!" he replied.

We shook hands and traded hugs as it would be a long time before we could expect to bump into each other. He was headed back to Fiji, so unless we ended up helping them clean up after another cyclone, or maybe another coup, it was unlikely we see each other again anytime soon. But we were optimists and we promised that we'd look each other up next time we were in town. Walking out of his room, I heard something that resembled the sound of a drunken walrus with a bad cough coming from Walker's room. The unmistakable sound echoed out of Watts' room and down the hall.

"Mate, you should get that looked at before you go," I offered, poking my head around the door.

Watts sprawled across one of the couches in the room as Walker meticulously packed his gear into his field trunk. Like the conscientious ex-digger that he was, Walker's room was neat, and his gear was laid out in an orderly fashion against his bed.

"Are you sticking around for BC day?" I asked.

"There's nothing wrong with being organized," he answered over his shoulder.

Walker was off to the infantry school next, and knew he'd be expected to hit the ground running.

"When are you blokes off?"

"Well, he's off in the next ten minutes, but you know me, I'm planning on being the last one out of here," replied Watts in his usual laid-back manner.

"Don't get caught being last, the last 1st class member has to pay all of the outstanding mess bills," I said with a grin.

"Really?!"

"Jesus, Watts, are you really that dumb?!" Walker said and shook his head.

Either way, Watts was in no hurry and would likely be here until dark. Which was fine by him as I knew he was planning on spending a few days in Canberra with his folks before following me down to Puckapunyal. He'd got his wish and been selected for Armored Corps, so he'd be heading down to 'tank school' around the same time as me.

"Well boys, what can I say. It's been swell, but the swelling has gone down. I'll see you blokes at a bar sometime soon," I said and gave them a left-handed salute.

"Anytime mate, you name the time and place, we'll be there," Walker replied and returned the comical salute.

I turned back to the hall and almost bumped into Hobbes as he was unsuccessfully attempting to haul his trunk and pack out of his room at the same time.

"As much as I'd like to sit here and watch you do this all day, do you need a hand?" I volunteered.

"Fuckin' oath!" he replied, his face already red from the exertion.

"You know, for a bloke going to transport, you really need to do a bit more planning," I said, grabbing a handle on his trunk.

"What do you mean?! This is military planning in action, now I've got you to do half the work!"

We carted his gear up to the carpark, swearing and cursing as the metal handles cut into our fingers.

"Righto, then mate, I guess I'll be seeing you in a couple of weeks," he said as he slammed the boot of his car closed.

"You bet. Don't do anything I wouldn't do in between now and then."

"Well, that does leave a lot to the imagination. I can't promise anything and will just have to do my best," he said with a grin and jumped into the car.

I slapped the top of his car and turned to go. At the other end of the carpark, I could see Heather trading hugs with her family as they went through the same routine. She waved back at me and I could see the relief on her face as she threw her pack into the back seat of her car.

I thought I'd drop by Alamein company and see if I could catch up Logan one last time. I knew I'd be seeing him again in the not-too-distant future, as he'd got his wish and was heading to the Artillery training school, which was also at Puckapunyal. Not that he was happy with it as the school had recently moved from north Sydney, where had views over the harbor and was within walking distance to a number of the best pubs in the city.

"Bloody hell mate, you look like I feel," I said when I got to his room.

"Yep, I reckon you could bottle of my sweat and sell it back to Dr Moose," he replied, his eyes still bleary from last nights' revelry.

"Where are you off to next mate?" I asked pulling up a chair amidst the chaos of his room.

"Up to the folks place on the central coast for a bit or R&R."

"I bet that beer garden at the Crown Plaza in Terrigal will get a work-out."

"Maybe, but not until the weekend... I need a few days of clean living."

We shook hands and I left him struggling to close the zipper on his ech bag, the back of his shirt stained with sweat and still smelling like rum.

"Oi, what are you doing?" EJ squeaked from her room as I walked down the hall.

"Same as you, I reckon. Getting out of here before they make me do another six months," I replied.

"Argghh, could you imagine it?! I reckon I'd die if I had to stay another day."

Her room looked like it had been turned upside-down and spun around a few times. Somehow, she'd managed to empty the contents of all of her cupboards onto each of the flat surfaces around the room.

"Looks like you'll be here till midnight at the rate you're going," I said and shook my head.

"Not bloody likely! Whatever doesn't fit in my bags is going in the bloody bin," she replied and threw her hands up.

"Well, better you than me mate. Anyway, I'm out of here. Don't forget to look me up if you need a hand assaulting the Mussorians or digging random holes in a hill sometime."

She gave me a hug and promised she'd look me up if she was ever in Darwin. I headed out of Alamein towards Kokoda to try and catch KD before he shot through. If there was one person who wanted to get out of the College more than me, it was KD.

"Have you blokes seen KD?" I asked the cadet I found in his room.

"Dunno, car park more than likely," one replied without looking up.

"Ripper, thanks," I said and ran off.

KD was off to the school of Signals for his next lot of training and was already looking forward to revisiting his old stomping grounds in Melbourne. Bolting up to the top carpark, I could see the boot up on his old Ford. I jogged over to find him cramming his pack into the front seat. The rest of the car was crammed full of what looked like the rest of his wardrobe.

"Nice packing mate," I said, resting my arm on the door.

"It's in and that's all that matters," he replied and slammed the door shut.

"That's not the first time I've heard that," I said with a laugh.

"Get stuffed. What are you doing here anyway?"

"Thought I'd come and see if you were interested in sticking around. It would be a shame to leave just when we've finally got the hang of this place."

We both grinned and shook our heads.

"There is not enough rum or money in the universe to make me even consider that idea," he replied.

"Well, I guess this is it for a while then mate."

"Looks like it. Give me a call when you get to Pucka and we'll sort out a weekend in Melbourne."

"Will do Mate. And hey, thanks for everything," I said and offered him my hand.

He stood up and looked at my hand briefly, one of his trademark grins starting to spread across his face.

"You don't need to thank me man. I couldn't have done it without you either."

We shook hands and patted each other on the back.

"Now, piss off and let me get out of here before someone figures out that I haven't handed in all of my pams!"

As I walked back to the Long Tan carpark, the sense of unease I'd felt earlier started to melt away. Even though a had a solid headache and my mouth still tasted like ouzo, I strolled along with my head up and a wry grin on my face. Amidst the noise and energy, I felt calm and removed from it all. I saw cadets hauling trunks and packs between buildings, the anxious looks on their faces evident under the strain of their loads.

"Better you than me fellas," I whispered.

I rounded the back of the military training wing building and almost walked into the Possum as he rounded the corner.

"Shit Poss, where did you bloody come from?" I said.

"Sorry mate. Had to go to the armoury to get my final signature. You all done?"

"Yeah mate, ready to roll. Pucka here we come." "Ahh well, have fun," he replied nervously.

"I will mate, you too. You heading back over the hill this afternoon?" I asked and leaned against the building.

"That's the plan. Another year of study though, you'd think I would have learned by now."

"You'll kill it mate. After all, you've made it through this place. Next year will seem like a holiday!" "I hope so," he replied.

The Possum was heading back to the Academy to finish his masters studies and would be heading to Signals once he was done. The College had been tough on him, but he'd clawed his way through, and you could sense the quiet pride he felt in having made it. Even though I could see the same person I knew from TEWTS, sword drill and field exercises, something about him had changed. His back was a little straighter, his shoulders were a bit squarer and his eyes were set with a firmness that I hadn't seen before. He knew he'd managed to survive everything that the College had thrown at him and was ready for whatever the Army had in store for him next. We patted each other on the back and headed our own way, not sure if we'd ever bump into each other again. Characters like the Possum were as much a part of the College as were the Drilly's, the parades and the hills of Majura. Amongst each class, there was always one or two that looked a little out of place or who seemed to have the odds stacked against them, but in the end most of them made it through. As I walked back in the direction of the carpark I wondered if that should be the unofficial motto of the College, "Struggled through, but made it in the end".

"Oi cadet, where do you think you are going?!" a loud voice behind me said as I was about to jump into my car.

I swung around to see Sergeant Ruth standing there with his pace stick tucked under his arm and a huge grin on his face.

"Wherever the hell I want, Sarge," I replied.

"You'll bloody keep. So, you're all done then are you?"

"Seems that way Sarge. Not that anyone would have guessed it six months ago."

"Well, you can say that again. Now, you've probably already heard this from the OC, but I'm going to say it again. When you get to your new unit, try and keep your bloody nose clean for a change. I know that is going to be almost impossible for you. But I'd like you to give it a go, because I'll be keeping an eye on you. Remember, it's the Sergeants who run this show," he said and shook his finger at me.

"I believe you Sarge. And thanks for looking after me, I didn't think I was going to make it if Zimburger had stuck around," I replied.

"You wouldn't have. He was itching to have you busted out of here. But between you and me, he was a bit of a prick and we're all glad to have him gone. Remember this though, there are plenty more like him out there. Officers and soldiers. You're not out of the woods by a long way. But for now, you're done here, so get going. I'll see you around... Sir," he said.

"Thanks, Sarge and maybe tomorrow you can call me Sir. But for now, let me get out of here first," I replied and thrust my hand out.

He shook my hand briefly, grinned and marched off in the direction of the company.

My car belched black smoke as the engine slowly spluttered into life. I let it settle into a steady rhythm before taking one last look around and pulling the door closed. Around me, the car park was almost empty as I dropped it into gear and rolled down the hill past the company. Through the windows I could see cadets setting up their rooms, drinking brews in the rec room and preparing themselves for the next stage of their journey. Part of me felt relieved to be leaving, while another part of me felt like I was leaving something behind. Somehow, I still felt like I was sneaking out of the place, even though I knew I had done all that it has asked of me. On my way to the gates, I drove slowly, taking it all in one last time.

Around me, the College watched me silently, content in the knowledge that I had done what it had asked. The parade ground, obstacle course and lecture halls were quiet, and seemed to ignore me as I passed them. The College had bid us farewell the moment we marched off the parade ground for the last time and would no longer concern itself with us, for its focus now rested solely on those that remained.

As it had done with us, it bore them no malice, nor did it expect any more or any less of them. In the same fashion it had done year after year, the College simply went about its job of turning young men and women into junior officers. It saw each new class as they entered its gates; fresh-faced, overconfident, yet eager to learn. It pushed and prodded them as they sweated and slogged their way through the challenges it had in store for them. It showed no favors to those who were stronger, smarter or wealthier than their classmates. When they got out of line, it pulled them up and pointed them back on the path it had planned. Most importantly, it made them work together to learn that they were stronger as a team than they could be as individuals.

Because it knew that when they left, they would be called on to lead soldiers to do things that the rest of the world could not or would not do. And it knew that this sort of leadership could not be taught in a classroom or textbook, nor did it simply appear along with a fancy job or title. The right to be a leader had to be earned and would only be given on those who understood that the real strength in any team was the trust and respect its members had for each other. So, it made sure that before they earned the right to be trusted as leaders, they first earned the right to be trusted as mates.

Epilogue

"Twenty years can seem like a really long time, or no time at all," KD said from behind me as he leant back in his chair.

Above us, the cloudless sky was filled with stars and the quiet of the night wrapped us in a cool embrace. The words lingered in the air and I strained my brain to think exactly where I had been twenty years ago.

"Hey, does anyone remember that bloody defensive exercise, what was it called again?" Woods said, his face illuminated by the firelight.

"You mean the one at Majura in the middle of winter?" Chuck said as he got up to grab a beer out of the esky.

"That's the one. I remember sometime around day three and we'd only managed to get our pit down to a foot and a half deep. Then it pissed down with rain and we ended up standing-to all night as the bloody thing filled up with water. Man, that sucked!" Woods added and shook his head.

"A foot deep? That would have been overhead for Chuck!" Cook chimed in from the other side of the fire.

"You're just jealous because you had to dig your pit ten feet deep to accommodate your massive head and nose!" Chuck said, returning fire.

The rest of us chuckled as we sifted through our own memories. Around the circle, the glow of the coals threw a warm orange light on our faces as we huddled around it, seeking protection from the cold air that ran down the from the mountains. As we did around the same time each year, we'd found a quiet spot in the country to get together and enjoy the company of our old classmates. With the fire on and a couple of beers in hand, it didn't take long before the years started rolling back. By the time the sun disappeared over the hills, the memories of field exercises, BC day inspections, bumph's, TEWTs and football games had regained their luster and we chipped each other for old indiscretions as if they'd happened only yesterday.

We sat around the fire until the early hours of the morning, pulling the piss out of each other and telling the same tall tales we told year after year. As the hours rolled by, the numbers slowly faded as we snuck off one by one to find our beds.

As the sun rose the next day, the joviality of the night before was replaced with grim faces and weary heads.

"I am never, ever, ever drinking with you blokes again," Dansen said, barely able to keep his eyes open.

"I bet you've given up smoking too," I added.

"Correct, add that to the list," he replied with a long sigh.

We were no longer the brave young Moose-warriors that we had been. Our ability to drink all night and bounce back for double-PT the next morning had been lost somewhere over the last twenty years.

"Fark, what happened last night," Mick said as he slumped down into the chair next to me.

"What do you mean, it still is last night!" Logan chipped in and the boys burst out laughing

Looking around the table, I could still see the traces of our youthful faces under the years. Sure, we were a bit heavier, a bit greyer and a bit slower around the track, but we were still the same young cadets at heart. Brash and self-assured, we reverted back to the twenty-year-old versions of ourselves each time we got together.

"Jesus Cook, you look even worse than you normally do," Dig said.

Cook's grim shape rolled out from under his swag and managed to look both puzzled and disgusted at the same time.

"I am never drinking with you blokes again," he said as he pulled a hanky from his pocket and wiped his brow.

"I think I've heard that before. Dansen, maybe you two could start a club," I replied with a grin.

The rest of us moved our chairs around to make room for him as he joined us. We spent the next few hours poking at the food on our plates and gingerly sipping our coffee. On occasion someone would reach across to pick the food off someone else's plate or pass their mug to someone who looked like they needed it more. Even though our heads hurt, and we were all dreaming of crawling back into bed, we felt at home again, safe in the company of our mates and memories.

"Well, what do you say? Another good year above ground and plenty more to come," Woods offered and raised his mug.

"Never grow up, never grow old," Chuck said from beside him.

"I'll drink to that," I added and raised my mug.

The sound of mugs and drink bottles clinking together echoed into the bush.

"Someone please tell me we're not doing this all again this afternoon?" Dig added wearily as he collapsed back into his chair.

"Afraid so mate, it's in the rules. Now who wants a breakfast beer?" Dansen chipped in, his red-faced contorted into a cheeky grin.

The reply was a bunch of blank faces and shaking heads.

Twenty years after marching out of the College, I wouldn't claim that my life was too much different to anyone else's. After graduating, we'd gone our separate ways as we headed off to different Corps, different postings and different lives. Over the years we'd juggled marriages, kids, houses, new jobs and a couple of wars in between. Like everyone else, I had my up days, down days and plenty of other days in between. On the whole life was just that, life. But every now and then, I'd find myself with more down days than up days. No matter how hard I tried, I couldn't get the needle to budge in the right direction. Anyone who's been there knows, it doesn't take too many of those days before the rot sets in. The light at the end of the tunnel would quickly disappear and I'd find myself carrying the weight of the world on my shoulders like a pack full of rocks. But, whenever it happened, one of my mates would appear. I don't know how they knew, but somehow, they did and when they saw me stumble, they would reach down to pull me back on my feet again.

So, when I look back at all the things I have learned and forgotten since my days at the College, the lesson that remains embedded in my memory is the first one that we learned, "look after your mates". All day, every day. While our faces may no longer be as fresh, nor our bodies as strong, the strength of the mateships that we forged at the College remain as strong as ever. Because we know, that when life gives you the blues, it's your mates that will get you through.

END.

Thanks

Firstly, a massive thanks to all of my mates who have helped me get through the many trials and tribulations that life has thrown at me over the last twenty odd years. I couldn't and wouldn't have done it without your help. Including plenty of times when I didn't think I needed it! Thanks especially to Chuck, Woods, Danny, Master, Dig, Espo, Mick, Sez, Viets, Ox, H, Bubski, Matt and even you, KD.

Secondly, thanks to my ever patient and persevering Mum. Without your continuous encouragement and support, I would never made it through the College, let alone get around to writing a story about it.

Lastly, no man is an island. Thank you Nevrie, for simply believing in me.
Always,
Rico

College Phrases, Acronyms and Military Terms

The art of speaking cadet.

BC Day – Battalion Commanders day or parade, occurs each Monday in barracks and involves a full inspection of every cadets room.

Bogging – cleaning, includes all manner of polishing, ironing, dusting, wiping and folding that cadets are expected to do to their equipment to get it up to standard.

Bumph – to be told off by one of the staff or senior cadets.

Cordy – A term used to refer to cadets who were members of the College or Defence Academy. A cordy, was by definition both a student and an officer in training and was expected to maintain the unwritten cordy traditions that were passed onto them by the classes that had gone before. Thought to originally come from a bastardisation of the word 'Corps'.

CSM – Company Sergeant Major, senior cadet in each company.

Dick-around – stuff around, waste time, or spend time doing useless things. Used to mean someone who wastes their time a lot but can also be used to indicate that you intend to waste someone else's time. Also substituted for 'Dick-about' by Army personnel from New Zealand.

Dressing – the way you or your personal equipment was aligned; in a group setting 'dressing' referred to the way the group was lined

College Blues

up, both when static and marching; for an individual, their uniform 'dressing' was the way that items in your uniform were aligned with the correct military dress standards. Dressing in a group was done using the markers, with everyone 'dressing' off the right marker in most instances.

Drilly – Drill Sergeant or member of the drill instruction wing. A senior soldier (Sergeant or Warrant Officer) responsible for instructing cadets how to conduct parade drill and instilling a sense of proper military bearing and/or decorum. Also responsible for delivering a continuous stream of bumph's at each parade practice.

DS – Directing Staff, name given to any of the instructors.

Dully – junior cadets, often referred to as dull due to their lack of knowledge. Also known as 'fourthies' due to the original degree course for officers being four years long.

DWSM – Drill Wing Sergeant Major, senior drill instructor.

Goffer – non-alcoholic cold drink, usually in a can. Most often from a vending machine, if you were lucky the 'Sally Man' would have them available during a break from field activities.

In-Step – the act of being aligned with your walking, running or jogging patterns i.e. both left feet at the same time, in cadence.

Marker – a tall person designated to stand at the end of a rank, who was then used to align everyone else in the rank during static or mobile drill. The markers were designated by the Drilly for each company, with one at the end of each rank (left and right markers).

OC – Officer Commanding, the officer in charge of a cadet company, usually an Army Captain (or equivalent where the role is filled by an exchange officer).

Paid-off – the act of not doing something, on purpose, with the express intent of avoiding the work and/or being too lazy to do it.

Pam/s – technical documents or booklets, usually in bound folders or small book format, that contain information on specific components of military service. Identified by a series of letters and numbers that represent the particular area they belong to.

Porto's – Short for port party, the name given to illegal drinking sessions in the lines. Thought to have originated from the practice of stealing the remaining port from one of the formal dining-in nights and taking it back to your room.

PMC – President of the Mess Committee, senior cadet position, leader of the color party and part of the Corps hierarchy.

PT – physical training, the name given for all forms of fitness training conducted in military service.

PTI – physical training instructor. A specialist breed of soldier, selected for their fitness, ability to yell continuously whilst conducting physical exercise and mis-pronounce surnames. Their role at the College was to ensure cadets reached the highest standards of physical fitness via the conduct of physical training and specialist PT advice such as, "Lean into the hill and let the hill do the work," and "Half of you over there, half over here and the other half, come with me!"

ROPs – Restriction of Privileges, a punishment whereby a cadet attends numerous parades each day in order to ensure they are still on barracks and their time is sufficiently 'dicked' around.

Round-about – the practice of being continuously in trouble, usually also associated with being on one of the 'shit lists".

RSM – Regimental Sergeant Major, the senior non-commissioned officer on barracks, responsible for drill and oversight of the CO's orders.

Schmick – to be in excellent condition, something or someone who is 'switched-on', looking sharp (clothing).

Shit list – an informal list kept by an instructor (or senior cadet) that identified those cadets who needed 'extra training' in response to them not conforming with the standards. Anyone on the 'shit list' would be the first ones picked for jobs or tasks that were unpleasant or designed to waste their time.

Split/s – the act of changing (splitting) into a different set of uniforms quickly. Often on the premise that it would teach you skills you'd need as an officer, such as managing your equipment and being ready at all times.

Stand-to – to prepare to defend your position, make ready for attack. For a cadet, this primarily meant lying down behind your weapon and trying not to fall asleep.

Square-away – being organized or to get organized, generally applied to a group of items, such as your room or your webbing but could also be applied to oneself.

Tap dance – to make something up, especially when in trouble. Not to be confused with lap-dance.

TEWT – Tactical Exercises Without Troops. These activities are the first step in learning how to command troops in battle and was conducted in the field using flags to mark positions (TEWT stakes) instead of real soldiers.

Walk-of-shame – to run out of money when in town and to walk back home (the College or anywhere). This generally happened as a result of getting to the point where you knew that you could either pay for another round of drinks or a cab ride home. Usually your mates convinced you that the drinks were a better option.

www.ingramcontent.com/pod-product-compliance
Lightning Source LLC
Chambersburg PA
CBHW020320010526
44107CB00054B/1910